WHAT CAN I EAT?

WHAT CAN I EAT?

A Family Guide to Allergy-free Cooking

Anne Clark

ANGUS
& ROBERTSON
PUBLISHERS

It appears to me necessary to every physician to be skilled in nature, and to strive to know, if he would wish to perform his duties, what man is in relation to the articles of food and drink, and to his other occupations, and what are the effects of each of them to every one.

Hippocrates 400-377 BC

ANGUS & ROBERTSON PUBLISHERS

Unit 4, Eden Park, 31 Waterloo Road,
North Ryde, NSW, Australia 2113, and
16 Golden Square, London W1R 4BN,
United Kingdom

First published in Australia by
Angus & Robertson Publishers in 1986
First published in the United Kingdom by
Angus & Robertson (UK) Ltd in 1986

National Library of Australia
Cataloguing-in-publication data.

Clark, Anne, 1947-
  What can I eat?
  Includes index.
  ISBN 0 207 15050 8.
  1. Food allergy — Diet therapy — Recipes.
  2. Gluten-free diet — Recipes.
  3. Sugar-free diet — Recipes. I. Title.
641.5'631

Illustrations by Lorraine Hannay

Typeset in 11 pt Bembo by Setrite Typesetters

Printed in Great Britain by
Richard Clay (The Chaucer Press) Ltd,
Bungay, Suffolk

CONTENTS

Acknowledgements

I wish to thank all those in the Armidale community who, by their frequent promptings and encouragement and our initial recipe sharing, have caused this book to come into being. To Sister Reeves and others at the Allergy Clinic I express my gratitude for their practical help in getting my family started with some basic recipes—some of which are included in this book. I am also deeply grateful to Dr Marjorie Davey for not only agreeing to write the Foreword to this book, but also finding time to evaluate the manuscript, particularly its medical aspects. Thank you also to Julie Gorrick of *Family Circle* for permission to reprint a number of recipes to demonstrate modifications.

I am also indebted to the two Armidale typists who came to my aid by typing the bulk of the manuscript, at short notice and within the deadline, after disaster struck my own type-writer.

Most importantly, I wish to say ''thank you'' to my family who put up with me before my food allergies were diagnosed, and then even more cheerfully put up with my culinary experimentation afterwards. They were even able to manage an encouraging ''yum'' to countless obviously in-adequate textures or tastes, or both!

Anne Clark

Foreword

A few years ago, Anne and some of her fellow citizens of Armidale discovered to their surprise that their ill health, chronic tiredness, fluctuations in emotions, lack of concentration and many other symptoms were not due to their "nerves", as they had been told. They had, at last, an explanation of why Valium and other tranquillisers made them feel worse, instead of better. Many of these people suffered from both hypoglycaemia and food allergies; the remainder had food allergies only. Though hypoglycaemia was more common in women, there were also male sufferers.

At that time, hypoglycaemia and, indeed, food allergies were not generally recognised as a cause of "nervous" symptoms. More recently, this concept has gained acceptance from some doctors, though many remain unconvinced. In Europe and the United States these conditions have been known for many years, and there is an extensive bibliography in almost every European language and in American publications.

Faced with the problem of coping with a radically different diet, the Armidale patients formed a hypoglycaemic group for mutual support and discussion. A survey of the group showed that there is a common symptomatology and that the symptoms of food allergy *per se* and hypoglycaemia frequently mimic each other. The group unanimously decided not to consider their problem as a disease. Rather, they saw it as an inability to cope with the excess sugar and refined carbohydrates in modern processed foods. The monotony of food in general, with reliance on one or two grains coming from a few species, exacerbated allergies. So did the addition of milk powders, yeast extracts, food colourings, etcetera, to many processed foods. This forced allergic people to read every label, looking for ingredients that could provoke allergic symptoms.

For the hypoglycaemics, the greatest difficulty was to avoid sugar, when nearly every available processed food (including soups, tinned meats, vegetables, cereals, etcetera) contains significant quantities of added sugar. All patients had to learn to cook with unusual grains and to substitute other ingredients, while providing palatable and nutritious food within the limits of their diet. This added up to one maxim— COOK YOUR OWN FOOD.

Anne led the group in responding to this challenge, and the result is this book of recipes, some collated by the group, but most created by Anne. Anne has addressed herself mainly to the problem of food allergies, but any hypoglycaemic reading this book will recognise that the recipes can, if necessary, be modified simply.

Watching this group become healthy, strong, happy, not "neurotic", and able to cope with life and enjoy it, has given me much satisfaction. Not the least of which was the lack of need for tranquillisers. The improvement in behaviour and performance of food-allergic children has been remarkable. The "proof of the pudding has been in the eating", which leaves no doubt that some illnesses, hitherto mysterious, are food related.

As well as to Anne, the book is a tribute to "patient power". It was born of the efforts of a group of people who knew that if they wanted to be well they had to find answers for themselves.

Marjorie E. Davey
MBBS BSc. (Melb.)
Armidale, NSW

INTRODUCTION

The common cry when you are confronted with a list of your allergies to common foods is "Whatever can I eat?". This bewildered feeling has been experienced by me, by my children, and has been related to me by those with food allergies who have come to me for help. To make matters worse, the change of diet is often sudden—one day the conventional diet, the next an allergy clinic visit and a new diet. The next few weeks then seem to be filled with anxious thoughts about what to eat for the next meal, and for the mother of an allergic child, how to produce enough variation so that the child will be willing to stick to the diet. This preoccupation continues until a "repertoire" of suitable recipes is established, by whatever means.

To the naturally inventive cook, a list of food allergies may be an exciting challenge rather than a problem. However, not everyone enjoys cooking to this extent. This book is written to help shorten the preoccupation stage and to ease the bewilderment of those having difficulty devising their own recipes. I would like to think that even inventive cooks may find the book useful—a few different ideas or just a short cut at extra-busy moments. Even though I have always loved cooking, there are moments in family life when to be able just to open a cookbook for a recipe is simply heaven.

Another aim of this book is to dispel the term "allergy

sufferer''. Once the particular dietary restrictions are adhered to, the individual should no longer be ''suffering'' from his/her particular allergy symptoms. The ideas in this book, then, dispense with the ''suffering'' of a restricted diet by showing how to prepare delicious food from unconventional ingredients. I myself have a long list of food allergies, but I certainly do not suffer. I feel more healthy and so much more alive than ever before and the alleviation of my past suffering is a great relief. Both myself and my children eat well. We show no tendency towards being overweight but are not thin either.

Each person's allergy pattern is different—both their symptoms and their range of allowable foods; this is a problem when writing a book of this nature. To open the book to a wider range of people, I have taken a ''workbook'' approach. As well as giving numerous tried and tested recipes, I have reprinted samples of recipes from magazines or recipes that are old favourites. I then show *how* I went about changing them according to the foods allowed—bread can be made without yeast, pastry without wheat flour, desserts without sugar and ice-cream without cow's milk. I wish to shake off any rigid ideas about what ingredients you *must* have to make particular recipes. Of course, many recipes will not produce exactly the same taste and/or texture as the one you are adapting—I do not boast to be able to get the same result with non-wheat flours as with wheat flour, for example, or to make creamy ice-cream with goat's milk. These things are not possible. What is possible, however, is to adapt recipes to produce delicious equivalents—equivalent in the sense that they can be used in the same way as the recipe you adapted. From my own experience and that of my children, if food allergies exist, then either (as with my youngest child at age three years) there is a natural aversion to foods you are allergic to, or there may be an addiction to the food and cutting it out will, at first, be associated with cravings and other withdrawal symptoms. However, in both cases, once you have become used to the adapted versions you will find them just as delicious but much more satisfying than the ones containing the allergy food.

Readers of this book will find certain guidelines that will

help them to "invent" their own recipes successfully, as they may not be as lucky as I was to have some hens which at least would give me some eggs from the wasted ingredients of my disasters in the early stages!

The recipes and ideas included in this book are free from cow's milk, yeast, added salt, cane sugar in all its forms, and use wholegrains exclusively. The book will, therefore, also be useful to hypoglycaemics, to which group I also belong. Diabetics, too, may find some recipes useful but should refer to their own guidelines before using these. Those people requiring not only a salt- and sugar-free but also a low-fat diet, are directed to *Cooking for Your Life* by Marlene Pentecost, Wattle Books, 1983.

The grains used in this book are exclusively wholegrains, of necessity for hypoglycaemics, but also because of my nutritional standpoint. On the Australian market, at least, wheat is the staple grain. Commercially available carbohydrate products—bread, biscuits, breakfast cereals and pastas—are made predominantly from wheat, either refined or wholewheat. Therefore, when you discover you are allergic to wheat it comes as a severe blow, and wheat *is* a common allergy food. Very little in the carbohydrate line can be bought in a ready-made form over the counter any more for such people. Some recipes using wholewheat flour are included, but the emphasis in this book is on *wheat-free* recipes, those that use the other grains—rye, oats, maize, buckwheat, rice—and the legume, soya flour, in whatever combinations are tolerated. Whole-wheat flour, compared to refined white flour, is relatively easy to handle, but the other grains have very different and individual properties so that straight substitution is not always successful.

The most urgent demand I receive from recently diagnosed allergic people is for a bread recipe, followed closely by recipes for cakes and biscuits, particularly in the case of children. Our eating habits may be only culturally determined but they are strong habits nevertheless and difficult to change in a hurry. In our society, breakfast usually means "cereal and toast" and the school lunch means "sandwiches". Hence I have included a comprehensive section on bread which will give a possible bread or roll alternative to anyone, providing they can tolerate at least one grain.

Another important section is on special occasions. Christmas, Easter and children's birthday parties can prove a real headache. The temptation tests the willpower of even the strongest person—and no child has willpower at a birthday party. If one has three allergic children in the family, what does one do? When my six-year-old's turn came to have a party this year, I gritted my teeth once again and devised alternatives to most of the commonly expected party fare. It was with a great sense of achievement (elation really) that I listened as one of the young guests sat down at the table and exclaimed with gusto, "Ah, party food." The food was eaten with similar gusto, proving that my efforts had been worthwhile. Commercial "no-no's" were not necessary; the allergic person need not "suffer" on festive occasions.

For those following the "rotary diet" approach to coping with multiple food allergies, I have included recipes for breads, pastries and cereals using different single grains or different combinations of grains so that rotation is possible. For the same reason, I specify simply "oil" in the recipes so that individual choice and/or rotation are possible.

Insofar as recipes in this book are free of cane sugar, salt, and artificial colourings, flavourings and preservatives, and use wholegrains, it may be considered a "health-food cookbook". However, this is more accidental than philosophical (I am not a health fanatic) and stems from the very *specific purpose of the book* —to help a well-defined group of people, those with food allergies and/or hypoglycaemia, to use a non-medical treatment for what for most of them has become a medical problem. My own philosophy on food, inevitably embodied in this book, has two facets: first, that only "real" (I prefer that term to "natural") food is eaten, hence nothing artificial is used and ingredients are as unprocessed as possible; and secondly, that each individual should be free to eat whatever makes him or her feel totally healthy, physically and mentally, however unusual these "real" foods may be. This book enables a person to be

8

free in a practical sense, and social freedom is something we all need to foster as part of our acceptance of the uniqueness of individuals.

In some sections the actual number of recipes may appear limited: this is because it is not my intention to supply an exhaustive range of recipes since other cookbooks are available to do just that. Rather, my aim is to provide only a suitable selection of recipes to illustrate ways of substituting other ingredients for the common allergy foods frequently found in cookbooks. You will then be able to delve back into your favourite recipe books and do your own adapting with the help of the guidelines given. For a comprehensive book on the subject, read *Recipes for Allergics* by Billie Little, Bantam Books, January 1983.

COOKING NOTES

Measurements

Recipes give cup measurements where possible. If metric quantities are used, imperial quantities are given in brackets. Conversions have been simplified for easy use in recipes. In any one recipe, use either imperial or metric quantities, but not a mixture of both.

Volume

1 cup = 250 ml or 8 fl oz
1 pint = 500 ml or 20 fl oz
4 cups = 1 litre or 32 fl oz
1 tablespoon = 20 ml ⎫ spoon measurements are
1 dessertspoon = 10 ml ⎬ slightly rounded unless
1 teaspoon = 5 ml ⎭ otherwise stated

Weight

30 g = 1 oz   250 g = 8 oz
100 g = 3 oz   500 g = 1 lb
125 g = 4 oz   1 kg = 2 lb

Temperature

Oven description	Celsius	Fahrenheit	Gas Mark
Very slow	120°	250°	½
Slow	150°	300°	2
Moderately slow	160°	325°	3
Moderate	180°	350°	4
Moderately hot	190°	375°	5
Hot	200°	400°	6
Very hot	230°	450°	8

Equipment

An electric blender is essential for milkshakes and for liquefying ingredients.

A juice extractor is essential for preparing fresh fruit and vegetable juices other than citrus juices. A citrus juicer is useful if citrus juice is used in large amounts.

A food processor aids considerably in making pastry, particularly with non-wheat flours, in mincing meat for sausages, chopping nuts and vegetables, and making purées. It speeds up the preparation time of most recipes. Most food processors have citrus-juicer attachments and some also have a general juice-extractor attachment.

A microwave oven, though still a luxury to most people, is the natural companion to a freezer. Small portions can be stored in the freezer and thawed in seconds in the microwave oven, making individual differences in food allergies within the one family easier to manage. Microwave cooking also greatly reduces the cooking time of some recipes, especially those with rye flour (see Rye-oat Soda Bread, p. 77, and Rye Flour Banana Loaf, p. 131).

Flour Quantity Conversions

The following amounts of the different flours each make 1 metric cup:

155 g (5 oz) rolled rice
125 g (4 oz) rice bran
155 g (5 oz) soya flour
185 g (6 oz) rye flour
220 g (7 oz) brown-rice flour
125 g (4 oz) rolled oats
155 g (5 oz) ground oats
155 g (5 oz) wholewheat flour
170 g (5½ oz) millet meal
125 g (4 oz) arrowroot flour
185 g (6 oz) buckwheat flour
185 g (6 oz) potato flour

Simplified metric/imperial conversions are:

60 g = 2 oz
90 g = 3 oz
125 g = 4 oz
155 g = 5 oz
185 g = 6 oz
220 g = 7 oz
250 g = 8 oz

Ingredients

Accompaniments

Make your own from the recipes given for basic sauces, dressings and gravies. Those available commercially frequently contain added sugar, salt, artificial additives, corn or wheat flour or other allergy-symptom-producing ingredients.

Arrowroot

Arrowroot flour is the very finely ground tuberous root of various plants. It is high in carbohydrates but does contain some vitamins and minerals. Use it as an alternative to cornflour as a thickener, but in smaller amounts. A combination of fructose and arrowroot is used in some recipes instead of the specified amount of sugar. It is also a useful binding flour for bread and other baking.

Baking Powder

Use sparingly for two reasons: it may contain cornflour and so is prohibited for those allergic to corn and it often contains compounds which accumulate in the body. It acts as a rising agent by releasing bubbles in the presence of water, or heat and water.

Bicarbonate of Soda

Also known as baking soda, bicarbonate of soda is the mineral compound, sodium bicarbonate. It is the main rising agent used in this book. Sodium bicarbonate is easily eliminated from the body.

Baking soda acts as a rising agent by releasing bubbles in the presence of an acid (for example, sour milk, yoghurt, some fruits and fruit juices). Used on its own, baking soda has an alkalising effect, which is undesirable since thiamine is destroyed by alkaline products. Use it in conjunction with an acid ingredient or cream of tartar (potassium acid tartrate)—the potassium counterbalances the sodium in the soda, which is useful information for those on sodium-restricted diets. The compound, sodium potassium tartrate, is formed with water and bubbles of carbon dioxide act as the rising agent. The alkaline soda is thus neutralised and is not harmful. Care should be taken to ensure that sufficient acidity is present to neutralise the soda. Err on the side of too much acid, rather than leaving some soda unneutralised. Crusts may not brown as readily if the product is more acid but this is about the only disadvantage.

See the introduction to Chapter 11: "Cakes and Slices", p. 123, for the proportions of bicarbonate of soda, and cream of tartar or soured milk, and for how to sour milk.

Butter

Butter is not used since the recipes are cow's-milk-free.

Carob

Carob powder is the dried and ground fruit of the carob tree. The fruit is also known as Saint-John's bread. Carob comes in dark or light powdered forms and is a useful cocoa alternative, although the flavours are certainly not identical. It is also available in block form like chocolate. Read the wrappers carefully for the other ingredients—they are frequently skim cow's milk and sugar.

Carob is naturally sweeter and does not have the bitter taste of cocoa, so added sweeteners may be decreased or even omitted when carob is used. This extra sweetness may prove too much for some hypoglycaemics so be wary in its use at first. Carob is low in calories and fat, compared with cocoa, and aids digestion.

Cheese

Goat's and sheep's cheeses are available for those allergic to cow's milk only. Cottage cheese, especially if homemade and therefore guaranteed fresh, may be more easily tolerated than hard cheeses. A recipe for junket-based goat's-milk cottage cheese is given on p. 87. Tofu is a soya-curd cheese for those allergic to dairy products. Those allergic to only the lactose in dairy products will often be able to tolerate cheeses and yoghurt but not straight dairy milk. Those allergic to yeast may react to the culture in most cheeses.

Cocoa

Chocolate and cocoa are common allergy foods, so carob is mostly used in this book. If cocoa is not on your allergy list, you may prefer to use it, often in lesser amounts than the amount of carob specified. Bear in mind that the oxalic acid in chocolate impairs the body's absorption of calcium. Cocoa has twice the calories of carob powder, and more fat.

Copha

Copha is useful to those who can tolerate only coconut-derived shortening. It is a purified form of coconut oil that can be used as a cooking medium or solidifying agent.

Cornflour

Cornflour may be used as a thickener if you are not allergic to corn. Use only pure cornflour—check on the packet to ensure it is made from maize. It is 90 per cent carbohydrate with virtually no vitamins or minerals.

Eggs

This is not a specifically low-cholesterol book, so egg yolks and whites are used. *Cooking for Your Life*, by Marlene Pentecost, is a book recommended for those needing a low-cholesterol diet as well as one that is sugar- and salt-free.

Egg Substitutes in Baking

To adapt your own recipes try the following egg substitutes:

• Egg powder
    250 g (8 oz) bicarbonate of soda
    100 g (3 oz) tartaric acid
    160 g (5 oz) cream of tartar
    7 g (¼ oz) powdered turmeric
    500 g (16 oz) ground rice

Thoroughly mix all the above ingredients and pass the mixture through a fine sieve. One teaspoonful to one dessertspoonful (according to recipe made) equals one egg. Mix into a small amount of warm liquid—it must effervesce—then add to the cake ingredients.

• Grated carrot is an excellent substitute for eggs when making boiled puddings. One small carrot, finely grated, is sufficient for a pudding for three persons.

• Gelatine mixture—one tablespoon of gelatine is equivalent to three eggs in a cake. Soften the gelatine in a little cold water. Add sufficient boiling water to make one cup (250 ml), then let the mixture cool until it has the consistency of eggwhite. Whip the mixture until light and add to the cake mixture.

See also p. 207 for an index of egg-free baking recipes.

Essences

Use only pure essences wherever possible. An alternative to pure vanilla essence, which may be difficult to obtain, is to use a vanilla bean—either stored in your jar of fructose to flavour the fructose, or heated with the milk in cooked custard-type puddings or cakes. Check the labels of commercial essences as they frequently contain sugar.

Flour

See the detailed introductory notes to Chapter 7: "Bread and Rolls", p. 69, for comments about the characteristics of the different non-wheat flours. Only wholegrain flours are used in this book because they are necessary for hypoglycaemics. With wheat flour, use stoneground if available: fine-ground for cakes and biscuits, baker's meal for breads. Store any flour bought in bulk in the freezer to prevent weevils or other deterioration.

Fructose

This is a fruit sugar; see "Sweeteners", p. 19.

Fruit

Preferably use fresh fruit in season, or frozen fruit; fruit tinned in natural unsweetened juice may also be acceptable. If a yeast allergy exists, care should be taken to ensure that the contents of a freshly opened tin is either consumed within 24 hours or the remainder frozen to prevent the development of an intolerable amount of yeast. Hypoglycaemics should bear in mind the amount of natural sweetness in these fruits and adjust amounts consumed accordingly.

Honey

See "Sweeteners", p. 19.

Kelp

Since salt is not used in the recipes, kelp powder is suggested as a source of the iodine necessary for healthy thyroid function. It would be advisable to check the iodine content of your drinking water with your local authority, since it is possible to ingest too much iodine. Kelp is a seaweed derivative available in powdered or granulated form: the powdered form is easier to slip into omelettes, bread, pastry, tomato sauce, etcetera, than the granules. The various brands taste quite different so change the brand if your family dislikes the first one tried.

Margarine

Several brands of milk-free (and mostly salt-free) margarine are available. This type of margarine is to be used in recipes if a cow's-milk-free diet is required.

Milk

Cow's milk is a common allergy food and all the recipes in this book are cow's-milk-free. Those who can tolerate cow's milk may use it, preferably skim milk, where milk is specified.

Goat's milk is now freely available, either from goat dairies, if you live in the country, or in the raw or pasteurised form from health-food stores (it is advisable to place an order, particularly in winter, to ensure supply), or in cartons from some supermarkets. It can simply replace cow's milk in all recipes except those relying on a high butterfat content, for example, ice-cream (extra margarine is added to goat's milk ice-cream).

The term "milk-free" in the recipes indicates that the recipe is dairy-free, that is, free of all dairy milk. If it is only cow's-milk-free, then this is specified as such.

Soya milk, being dairy-free, can be a good substitute for dairy milk (and is often cheaper, in the powdered form, than goat's milk) and may be used in baking. It is a good protein source, being derived from soya beans. Check from the label or with the storekeeper that the powder is grain-free and sugar-free. Some soya-milk powders contain wheat and/or corn and/or lactose.

Mould

Particularly if an allergy to mould exists, use only very fresh ingredients or freshly opened tinned foods. Mushrooms should be avoided. Preserve excess or left-over food promptly by freezing it in suitably sized amounts.

Nuts

Nuts may be bought in bulk from some health-food wholesalers —a saving if nuts are used a lot. Store the excess in the freezer to preserve freshness. Several pure nut butters, free from artificial additives, sugar and salt, are now available from health-food shops, for example, almond, hazelnut, cashew, peanut (a legume, not a nut) and also seed butters, such as sesame seed. Use seeds or beansprouts as a substitute for nuts.

Oil

Use any allowable pure liquid oil when a recipe specifies oil. Be wary of oil blends unless you can be sure which oils (and hence which grains or seeds) are in the blend.

Peanuts

Strictly speaking, a legume and not a nut; see "Nuts", p. 18. They can be bought roasted and unsalted.

Salt

Research consistently points to the contribution of salt intake to high blood pressure, so no salt is used in these recipes. Many foods have a high sodium content anyway, so extra sodium from the use of table salt is unnecessary nutritionally. Herbs and spices are used in the recipes to enhance the flavour of the food, allowing those who do not wish to use salt to avoid it, and encouraging others to omit it. Obviously it may be added by those who are not yet used to salt-free foods.

Soya Milk

See "Milk", p. 17.

Sugar

See "Sweeteners", below.

Sweeteners

No cane sugar or artificial sweeteners are used in these recipes, but several sweetener options are given. Choose sweetener substitutes according to your needs if a recipe is not sweet enough with the natural sweetening in fresh or dried fruit or juices.

Fructose is a fruit sugar tolerated by many hypoglycaemics. Use it in small amounts only because of its strong sweetness—a maximum of about 1 tablespoon per cake.

Honey may be tolerated, in small amounts, by hypoglycaemics and those with food allergies.

Sultanas (or other dried fruits) contain fructose and glucose, a combination which may be better tolerated by some hypoglycaemics than straight fructose. Liquefy them to release the sweetness through foods. Store dried fruit in the refrigerator to help retain freshness. If you are hypoglycaemic, limit the quantity of dried fruit eaten, if necessary.

Mannitol is a six-carbon sugar, prepared commercially by the reduction of dextrose. It is virtually inert metabolically in humans, and occurs naturally in fruits and vegetables such as olives, onions and mushrooms. It is available in powdered form under various brand names. It can cause flatulence and abdominal pain in some people, so use it in modified amounts.

Equal is the brand name of a sweetener derived from amino-acid components like those found naturally in foods. It is available in tablet or powdered form and can be used to sweeten any uncooked foods. It contains phenylalanine so must not be used by phenylketonurics.

Tea and Coffee

Not suggested here because of the number of people allergic to them. Coffee substitutes are available from health-food stores, but check the labels carefully for other allergy foods. Numerous herb teas are available from health-food stores and may be bought in bulk, packet or individual sachet form. I recommend starting with spearmint, which is also very refreshing chilled on a hot summer's day (milder than peppermint); lemon grass for those who like a lemon flavour; basil and borage as a daytime savoury tea; and hawthorn tea. Be aware that herb teas may not be tolerated either despite their supposedly "healthy" connotations.

Tofu

This creamy soya curd is useful as a bland base for dips, creams, spreads, and so on.

Check the ingredients on the label of commercial tofu for salt, etcetera. A recipe for tofu (Soya-bean Cheese) is given on p. 88.

Vegetables

Preferably use fresh vegetables or freeze your own surplus. Commercially frozen vegetables may contain sugar, salt, colouring or other additives.

Yeast

No baker's or brewer's yeast are included in the recipes as these are common allergy foods; bicarbonate of soda is the main alternative rising agent used. Natural yeasts may develop in tinned and bottled foods and juices after opening so refrigerate these foods if not eaten immediately, or freeze them if they are not to be consumed within a short period of time.

Yoghurt

Goat's yoghurt, both plain and sweetened, is available from health-food stores and some supermarkets. The bacteria in yoghurt are beneficial to the digestive system. Because it is predigested by these bacteria, yoghurt may be tolerated by those who cannot tolerate the lactose in fresh milk, but not by those allergic to milk protein. Those with an allergy to yeast or mould may not tolerate the culture in yoghurt. Being an acid food, yoghurt can be used, when baking with bicarbonate of soda, to neutralise the soda, instead of adding lemon juice or cream of tartar.

1
BEVERAGES

For those able to tolerate goat's or soya milk:

Protein Shake

   2 cups goat's or soya milk
   1 teaspoon lecithin
   ½ teaspoon vanilla essence
   1 egg
   1 dessertspoon sultanas or 1 dessertspoon carob powder

Blend all the above ingredients at high speed until frothy.
Makes about 2½ cups.

Basic Creamy Milkshake

3 cups chilled goat's or soya milk
1 cup iced water
1 large or 2 small frozen bananas, roughly sliced
1 teaspoon vanilla essence (or to taste)

Place all the above ingredients in an electric blender and blend on high speed until frothy—the banana produces the creaminess. Increase the amount of banana if a more prominent banana flavour is desired. Makes about 5½ cups.

To vary this recipe, add any of the following:

- 1 dessertspoon of carob powder—a family favourite;
- ½ cup of coconut;
- 1 dessertspoon of walnuts;
- any combination of these.

Gavin's Pink Refresher

2 cups (16 fl oz) chilled goat's milk
2 cups (16 fl oz) chilled watermelon pieces (seeds and skin discarded)
2 tablespoons coconut (or to taste) (optional)

Blend all the above ingredients at high speed until smooth. This is a very thirst-quenching drink and a beautiful colour—my son's invention one day when we ran out of strawberries. Makes about 4½ cups.

Strawberry Almond Milk

2 cups chilled goat's milk
1 cup hulled washed strawberries
1 heaped tablespoon toasted blanched almonds

Blend all the ingredients in an electric blender until smooth. Makes 3 cups.

For those unable to have fresh milk but able to have yoghurt, try this:

Maree's Yoghurt Shake

1 egg per person
1 cup natural yoghurt per person
honey to taste or Equal or fructose
1 dessertspoon lecithin granules per person
1 teaspoon vanilla essence per person
Generous amount of fruit to taste, fresh or stewed, e.g. bananas,
*   strawberries, apricots, stewed apple, or carob powder to taste*

Place all the ingredients in an electric blender and blend until smooth.

Fresh Fruit Juice

If you have a juice extractor, fresh fruit juices depend only on the contents of your fruit bowl and your whim.

Useful additions to fresh fruit juice are:

• A sprinkling of vitamin C powder, approximately ¼ teaspoon per glass, will prevent fresh apple juice turning brown although the froth on top may still brown, but may be skimmed off. The juice will retain its fresh colour for several days, though fresh juices should always be consumed as soon as possible after preparation. Vitamin C powder comes as sodium ascorbate or calcium ascorbate (useful to those wishing to decrease their sodium intake).

• Added mineral water gives a lemonade-fizz effect to juices for children—apple, orange, apricot, or pineapple; and a pre-dinner sparkle effect for adults. Alter the proportions of mineral water and juice according to your personal preference.

• Add fresh mint to apple or pineapple juice for a refreshing change. If fresh mint is not available, add some freshly made then cooled spearmint tea (*note*: not peppermint tea).

Festive Fruit Punch

850 ml (30 fl oz) unsweetened tinned or fresh apple juice, chilled
2 cups freshly poured, cooled spearmint tea
1 cup watermelon balls or cubes
750 ml (26 fl oz) chilled mineral water

Combine the first three ingredients and mix well. Just before serving, pour the mixture into a clear bowl, add the mineral water and float some fresh mint sprigs on top.

If juicing your own apples, choose the variety according to the sweetness desired: Granny Smith's produce a sharp clean apple flavour; Delicious or similar produce a sweeter flavour. Serves 8-10.

Vegetable Juice

Have you tried fresh vegetable juice as a cleansing aperitif or a mid-morning pick-me-up? If the idea has never appealed to you, try the following progression gradually:

• Apple and carrot juice—mix equal quantities of each—a popular transition.
• Carrot and a small amount of celery—a savoury juice.
• Carrot, celery and raw fresh beetroot—surprisingly sweet and a ruby colour.

Hot Carob Drink

Use carob powder with goat's or possibly soya milk as you would for cocoa—about 1 teaspoon carob per cup of milk, or to taste—for a nutritionally superior drink. See "Cocoa" under "Ingredients", p. 14.

Other possible beverages may be found in most cookery books. Substitute goat's or soya milk for cow's milk in milk drinks, if necessary, and use fresh juices from your juice extractor, unless the unsweetened pure tinned juices are tolerated. When deep-freezing goat's milk, keep these points in mind:

- Once it leaves the goat, the milk should be cooled and frozen in the absolute minimum of time, so that the cream does not rise.
- It must be kept at 0°C (32°F). The temperature must not be raised at any time while the milk is stored, as, even if lowered again, the milk will thaw in flakes which look unattractive, though it is really not harmed.
- Provided the temperature is kept constant, the milk can be kept for about six weeks.
- Thaw naturally—do not heat or stand in hot water to thaw.
- After thawing, the milk will keep in the refrigerator for about 2-3 days, but it is always best consumed as quickly as possible.

2
STARTERS

Sausage Nibbles

Prepare homemade sausages according to recipes given in Chapter 5, pp. 59-61. Pan-fry or grill until cooked. Chill, then slice into chunks for nibbling on their own, or else to be first dipped in your own prepared tomato sauce (pp. 33 and 45) with toothpicks, or in a cottage-cheese-based dip (recipes follow).

See also the suggestion about sausage rolls in the introduction to the pancake section, p. 98.

Dips

Mix thoroughly with desired quantity of goat's-milk cottage cheese (recipe p. 87) or tofu (recipe p. 88), any of the following. Chill well before using.

• Caraway, poppy or toasted sesame seeds.
• A generous quantity of herbs, preferably fresh, for example, parsley, marjoram, dill, chives, basil, with a little grated onion.
• Spices such as cumin and coriander for a mild curry taste, with a little grated or minced onion and finely chopped celery, or for a sweet curry taste, liquefy 1 tablespoon of sultanas with the cottage cheese in an electric blender and then add the spices. Alternatively, add thick stewed apple in place of the sultanas.

Crispbreads

Pure-wheat or pure-rye crispbreads are available and are useful, suitably topped, as hors d'oeuvres. Matzos are large wheat-flour and water only wafers, available also in wholewheat. Cut them to an appropriate size for hors d'oeuvres or break into pieces for dips. Alternatively, use commercial rice-cakes made from brown rice, unsweetened recrisped waffles or waffle segments made from the grain you can tolerate; see Chapter 9, p. 94.

Always top crispbreads immediately before serving as they soften quickly once spread. The following recipe and variations may be used as toppings for crispbreads.

Mock Chicken

> 1 tablespoon margarine
> 1 tablespoon chopped onion
> 1 skinned and chopped tomato
> 1 teaspoon mixed herbs
> 1 beaten egg
> parsley to garnish

Melt the margarine and fry the onion until soft but not browned. Add tomato and mixed herbs and simmer for approximately five minutes until the mixture is softened. Add the beaten egg and stir until mixture thickens, remove from heat and add chopped parsley. Chill before using. Makes ¾ cup.

To vary this:

• Try ½ teaspoon ground oregano instead of mixed herbs.
• Spread crispbread with goat's-milk cottage cheese (see recipe p. 87) mixed with chopped celery and walnuts.
• Spread with scraping of margarine then sliced hardboiled egg, tomato and sprinkle with finely chopped chives.
• Spread with Tomato Spread: an egg-free recipe (see p. 90).

Savoury Cases

To make these you need a special savoury-case iron as shown in Figure 1 on p. 30. There are several brands available through large department stores or speciality kitchenware shops. Each comes with one or more attachments of which the rosette shape is the one I use most.

If the grains in the following batter alternatives do not suit, try substituting any allowable grains in the wheat-flour recipe, for example, rye, millet, buckwheat, with or without some potato or arrowroot flour.

If the cases are to be used as sweet cases, omit the kelp and add 1 teaspoon of fructose or honey to the batter if allowed.

Wheat Flour Batter

> 2 eggs
> pinch kelp powder (optional)
> 1 cup goat's or soya milk
> 1 cup 100 per cent wholewheat flour

Beat the eggs gently then add the remaining ingredients. Continue beating until the mixture is smooth. Use as shown below. Makes 24 cases.

Rye-soya Flour Batter

> 2 eggs
> pinch kelp powder (optional)
> 1 cup goat's or soya milk
> ½ cup whole-rye flour
> ½ cup full-fat soya flour

Beat the eggs gently then add the remaining ingredients. Continue beating until the mixture is smooth. Use as shown below. Makes 24 cases.

Soya-rice Flour Batter

2 eggs plus 1 eggwhite
pinch kelp powder (optional)
¾-1 cup goat's or soya milk
½ cup brown-rice flour
½ cup full-fat soya flour
½ cup rice bran (polishings)

Beat the eggs gently then add the remaining ingredients. Continue beating until the mixture is smooth. Allow the batter to stand for 30 minutes to thicken and soften—it should be quite thick as these soya-rice cases are fragile. Use as shown below. Makes 24 cases.

Figure 1 Cookery method for savoury cases.

To cook all the above batters, melt 250 g (8 oz) of copha in a small saucepan. Heat gently until a drop of batter sizzles when put in the copha. Screw on the desired attachment to the iron and immerse in the hot copha to heat the iron. Dip the iron into the prepared batter then immerse in the hot copha. The savoury case is cooked when it turns a pale golden colour. Remove from the copha, gently prize the case off the iron (a matchstick or a pointed knife is useful to poke in the corners) and cool on a wire rack. The first few cases may not come off cleanly if the correct temperature and batter consistency have not been obtained, but persistence is worthwhile. The cases may be made well in advance and stored in airtight containers.

To use, place the empty cases on a flat tray and reheat at 180°C (350°F) for approximately 20 minutes or until crisp. Fill, while hot, with the desired savoury filling:

Savoury Fillings

For 24 cases, use 1½-2 cups of savoury filling.

• Sauté finely chopped or minced left-over meat with some finely chopped onion. Add a peeled and chopped tomato, oregano to taste and a little chopped parsley. Add a small amount of water, simmer for 10 minutes, then thicken with a little arrowroot to a fairly stiff mixture.

Make a thick white sauce (see recipe p. 44) and add your choice of:

• Chopped and sautéed onion and green pepper; chopped left-over chicken pieces and finely chopped parsley.
• Tuna, chopped parsley and finely diced red pepper for colour (optional). Add a dash of paprika, ½ teaspoon coriander, ¾ teaspoon cumin and a squeeze of lemon juice.
• Chopped cooked spinach or silver-beet leaves and chopped hardboiled eggs. Season with black pepper and finely chopped chives if desired.

Pizzas

Make pizzas on rectangular oven trays, cut into small finger-length strips and serve warm with pre-dinner drinks or as party savouries.

Alternatively, make pizzas on the traditional round ovenware plate or tray, cut into wedges and serve as an entrée or a luncheon dish with salad and bread rolls.

Non-wheat Pizza Dough

½ *cup brown-rice flour* ⎫ or *other* ⎫ or *1½ cups plain*
½ *cup rice bran* ⎬ *tolerated* ⎬ *wholewheat*
½ *cup soy flour* ⎭ *flours* ⎭ *flour*
½ *teaspoon bicarbonate of soda*
1 *teaspoon cream of tartar*
½ *teaspoon paprika*
1 *teaspoon kelp powder (optional)*
¼ *cup margarine*
½ *cup water* or ½ *cup goat's* or *soya milk with juice of half a lemon added*

Sift dry ingredients together into a bowl, then rub in margarine. Mix in water or milk-lemon juice mixture to form a soft dough. Pat out, using floured fingers, onto a lightly oiled tray. Brush a small amount of oil over surface of the dough and cover with 1-1½ cups of Italian-style Tomato Sauce (recipe follows). Makes one 33 cm (13 in) diameter round tray.

Italian-style Tomato Sauce

1 medium chopped onion
1 tablespoon oil
2 sticks celery
500 g (1 lb) skinned and chopped tomatoes
1 medium peeled and sliced apple
½ cup water
½ teaspoon marjoram or oregano (or to taste)
black pepper to taste (optional)

Sauté the onion in the oil, then add remaining ingredients and simmer uncovered for 20 minutes. Purée mixture in a food processor or blender for a smoother sauce. Makes 3 cups.

Cover tomato sauce with one of the following or your own choice:

Bolognese Pizza

Meat Sauce
500 g (1 lb) lean minced beef
1 finely chopped medium onion
1 dessertspoon oil
1 finely chopped stick celery
1 peeled and chopped medium tomato
1 cup water or vegetable stock
¼-½ teaspoon oregano (or to taste)
black pepper to taste
1 dessertspoon arrowroot

Brown the beef and onion in the oil. Pour off excess fat, and add the remaining ingredients, except arrowroot. Cover and simmer for 30 minutes, then thicken with arrowroot mixed to a paste with a little cold water. Spread the meat sauce over the tomato sauce then top with plain goat's cottage cheese or tofu. Bake in the oven at 190°C (375°F) for 30 minutes or until the crust is cooked and the top is golden.

Green Pepper and Onion Pizza

1 medium sliced onion
½ cup sliced celery
¾ cup sliced green pepper
1 tablespoon oil

Sauté onion, celery and green pepper in the oil until softened but not browned. Spread this mixture over the tomato sauce. Top with sliced tomato, and, if allowed, sliced mushrooms and bacon strips (both optional). Spread goat's cottage cheese or tofu over the top. Bake in the oven at 190°C (375°F) for 30 minutes or until the crust is cooked and the top is golden.

Cheese-free Pizzas

If no milk products are tolerated, a beaten egg may be substituted for any cheese toppings, giving a similar golden "melted" appearance and added protein.

In the Bolognese Pizza recipe above, prepare the pizza up to the stage of spreading the meat sauce. Then bake the pizza at 190°C (375°F) for 20-25 minutes. Remove from oven, top with two beaten eggs, then return pizza to oven and cook until the eggs are set and the crust is cooked.

In the Green Pepper and Onion recipe above, leave out the cottage cheese layers. Bake pizza as directed until the crust is almost cooked, remove from oven and top with two beaten eggs. Return pizza to oven until crust is cooked and the eggs are set.

Alternatively, if only one family member is allergic to cheese, leave a portion of a family-sized pizza free from cheese and simply pour the beaten egg over this section. It will confine itself well enough to the desired portion and makes it possible to cook just one pizza for the whole family.

Sweet and Spicy Pizza

Spread Sweet 'n' Spicy Tomato Sauce (see recipe p. 45) over crust instead of the Italian-style Tomato Sauce. Spread this with 1 cup goat's cottage cheese or tofu. Top with stoned and halved prunes and slices of red pepper for garnish, or bacon strips if tolerated. Bake as for Bolognese Pizza.

In any of these pizzas, sliced firm goat's or sheep's cheeses may be used in place of the cottage cheese, if tolerated.

Cocktails

Rockmelon (Cantaloupe) Cocktail

1 ripe halved rockmelon, seeds discarded
1 teaspoon (or to taste) finely chopped fresh mint
2 tablespoons boiling water
2 tablespoons extra water or unsweetened apple juice

Scoop out the flesh from the rockmelon with a melon-baller. Steep the mint in the boiling water and cool. Place melon balls in a bowl and pour over the mint mixture and extra liquid; stir thoroughly. Chill for several hours in the refrigerator, stirring occasionally. Serve in small glass bowls, garnished with a sprig of mint. Serves 4-6.

Pineapple Cocktail

As above, but substituting fresh pineapple diced into small wedges. The smaller, "rough" pineapples are a more golden colour and very sweet. Garnish with a whole strawberry.

Starters

Stuffed Capsicums

3 *large green* or *red peppers*
100 *g (3 oz) diced raw potato* or ½ *cup cooked brown rice*
2 *tablespoons sunflower seeds*
1 *tablespoon oil*
1 *thinly sliced onion*
500 *g (1 lb) peeled and chopped tomatoes*
½ *teaspoon oregano*
good pinch chilli powder
2 *tablespoons fresh corn kernels* or ½ *cup early mung bean-sprouts*
1 *tablespoon sultanas (optional)*
60 *g (2 oz) coarsely grated cheese (goat's* or *sheep's)* or *beaten egg* or *omit both*

Cut peppers in halves lengthways. Discard core and seeds. Steam halves for 10 minutes to soften, then drain and set aside. Steam potato dice until just tender, then drain. Meanwhile, toast sunflower kernels carefully in a dry saucepan over medium heat until just golden. Heat the oil in a saucepan, add the onion and cook until soft but not brown. Add all remaining ingredients except the cheese (or egg). Cover saucepan and simmer the mixture until thickened. Stir in the rice or cooked potato, and sunflower seeds. Spoon the mixture into the pepper halves and top with grated cheese or beaten egg. Cook under a hot griller until cheese is golden or egg set. Serve immediately. Serves 6.

Pineapple-stuffed Tomatoes

6 medium tomatoes

125 g (4 oz) chopped cooked ham (sugar-free ham with lower sodium content)

¾ cup chopped fresh pineapple or chopped unsweetened tinned pineapple

¼ cup chopped walnuts

¼-½ cup dressing, e.g. Boiled Salad Dressing (p. 44) or goat's yoghurt, or goat's cottage cheese creamed and thinned with extra goat's milk or tofu, with 1 teaspoon lemon juice added

chopped parsley

Cut a slice from the top of the tomatoes; scoop out pulp and chop, then drain the tomatoes upside down. Mix ham, pineapple, walnuts and sufficient chopped tomato to fill the tomato cases well. Add dressing to mixture then spoon into tomato cases and chill well; garnish with parsley. Use as a starter to a meal, or salad accompaniment for a buffet meal, luncheon or barbecue. Serves 6.

Savoury Tarts (*Quiches*)

Serve savoury tarts in small wedges, garnished with finely sliced lettuce and a sprig of parsley, as an entrée. Serve larger portions, with side salad and fresh bread, for a luncheon. Take cold tarts as a treat on a special picnic, or add a left-over slice in a school lunch.

Many vegetables may be used in these quiches. The following are popular with my family but try your own combinations according to what is in season. Add your favourite herbs if desired. For pastry-flan case recipes using different grains, see Chapter 9, p. 104. The quantities given in the following recipes are for a generous-sized tart, 27 centimetres (10½ in) in diameter. Quiche portions freeze well so it can be a time-saver to make the larger quantity. The same quantities will make two smaller 18-centimetre (7-in) flan cases.

Onion and Tomato Tart

 1 pastry case, 27 cm (10½ in) diameter, uncooked or baked blind
   for 10 minutes
 1½ tablespoons oil
 2 large sliced onions
 4 eggs
 1½ cups goat's or soya milk
 chopped parsley
 black pepper to taste
 3 sliced tomatoes

Sauté onions in the oil until transparent; place onions in pastry
case. Beat eggs, then add milk, parsley and pepper. Pour egg
mixture over onions and arrange sliced tomatoes gently around
the edge. Cook at 210°C (425°F) for 15 minutes, then turn
oven to 160° (325°F) for 40-45 minutes or until filling is just
set. Serves 6.

Spinach Tart

 1 pastry case, 27 cm (10½ in) diameter, uncooked or baked blind
   for 10 minutes
 1 tablespoon oil
 1 large finely sliced onion
 5 large leaves silver beet or equivalent amount true spinach
 4 eggs
 1 cup goat's or soya milk
 ½ teaspoon kelp powder (optional)
 black pepper to taste
 finely chopped chives

Heat oil in a small pan and sauté onion gently until softened but
not browned. Meanwhile, trim silver beet leaves off stalks, or
any coarse ends off spinach; wash leaves thoroughly, then place
them in a saucepan with ¼ cup water over a medium heat.
Steam until soft (5-10 minutes) then drain. Purée leaves, then
add to the eggs beaten with milk and seasonings. If you possess
a food processor, place drained cooked leaves in the processor

and chop finely. Add milk, eggs and seasonings and process briefly until blended.

Pour spinach mixture over onion in pastry case. Leave plain or garnish with a few tomato slices or red pepper strips. Bake in oven at 210°C (425°F) for 15 minutes then reduce heat to 160°C (325°F) for 40-45 minutes or until filling is just set and puffed. Serve immediately, accompanied by warm Tomato Sauce (recipes p. 33 and p. 45). Serves 6.

The title is something of a misnomer in Australia as silver beet is commonly used in place of the true spinach.

Winter Tart

> 1 pastry case, 27 cm (10½ in) diameter, uncooked or baked blind for 10 minutes
> 1 large sliced onion
> 1 tablespoon oil
> 1 cup newly sprouted mung beansprouts or fresh corn kernels
> 200 g (6 oz) broccoli, preferably fresh
> 4 eggs
> 2 cups goat's or soya milk
> black pepper to taste
> fresh majoram and finely chopped parsley (optional)

Sauté onion gently in oil until softened, then spread onion over base of flan case. Lightly steam broccoli until just tender; chop coarsely and spread over onion in case. Sprinkle over mung beansprouts or corn. Beat eggs and milk, then add seasonings and pour mixture over the vegetables. Bake in a preheated oven at 210°C (425°F) for 10 minutes then reduce temperature to 160°C (325°F) for remaining 30-40 minutes or until the crust is cooked and the filling is just set and puffed. Serve with Tomato Sauce (pp. 33 and 45) if desired. Serves 6.

Soups

Homemade soups are quick to make, as well as being cheap, delicious and very adaptable for those on a restricted diet. An electric blender produces a more velvety soup than a food processor, but a food processor can speed up the chopping preparation.

Save any liquid from steaming vegetables as vegetable stock and always use this or meat stock in preference to water for flavour and nutritional value when making soup. Prepare your own meat stocks and store in cup-sized or larger containers in your freezer for a quick soup base. My favourite method for cooking a boiling hen keeps us amply supplied with pure chicken stock. Simply place the completely thawed or fresh bird in a large casserole or Dutch oven, fill to three-quarters full with water and place lid on tightly. Bake at 120°C (250°F) for 2½ hours. Chill chicken and liquid, then lift off fat. Use the chicken in recipes such as Chicken Mornay, p. 54, and the liquid for sauces and soups.

For beef stock, simmer some soup bones for one hour (usually packaged as such at supermarkets, or from your butcher) with a little chopped onion, celery stalk or tops, carrot, a bay leaf, a few peppercorns and water to cover. Strain, chill so solidified fat can be lifted off, and freeze any surplus.

Soups may be adapted for allergies in a number of ways:

• Substitute goat's milk freely for cow's milk. Try out your recipes with soya milk too.
• A creamy soup, without cream, can be made using a white sauce as a base, but using stock rather than milk. Possible thickening agents to choose from, for the sauce are: cornflour, arrowroot, potato flour or brown-rice flour. Refer to Chapter 3, p. 43, for characteristics of these.
• If you are allergic to potatoes, substitute 1 heaped tablespoon of uncooked brown rice for one medium potato. When puréed, the soup will be just as thick.

To illustrate, here are two generally popular soups.

Zucchini (Courgette) Soup

1 tablespoon oil
1 sliced onion
1 medium peeled and thinly sliced potato or 1 heaped tablespoon
uncooked brown rice
6 medium zucchinis (about 1 kg or 2 lb)
1-2 teaspoons dried tarragon leaves
4 cups chicken stock
freshly ground black pepper to taste

Cut the zucchini into thick slices. Heat the oil gently in a large
saucepan, add the onion, potato and zucchini and sprinkle with
tarragon and pepper. Cover and cook over a low heat for 10
minutes, shaking the pan from time to time, but do not allow
the vegetables to brown. Add stock and simmer, covered, for
20 minutes. Sieve soup or purée in a blender or food processor.
Serve hot or chilled. Serves 6-8.

Cream of Cauliflower Soup

1 fresh or frozen cauliflower (about 1 kg or 2 lb)
4 tablespoons margarine
4 tablespoons flour for thickening (see above for options)
4 cups chicken stock
1 coarsely chopped onion
1 chopped stalk celery
2 chopped sprigs parsley
freshly ground black pepper and nutmeg to taste
2 egg yolks ⎫
½ cup goat's or soya milk ⎬ *(optional enrichment)*

Break the cauliflower into florets and lightly steam for five
minutes, then drain. To make the sauce base, melt the
margarine in a saucepan, add the chosen flour and cook, stirring
continuously, until a smooth paste is formed. Add chicken
stock gradually, stirring until the mixture is smooth. Add
onion, celery, parsley and cauliflower and simmer until
cauliflower is softened, taking care that the soup does not catch

on the bottom (this easily happens with flour-based soups). Purée the soup in a blender, then reheat, stir in the egg yolks and/or milk (if used). Season with pepper and a little freshly grated nutmeg and garnish with parsley—a hearty soup. Serves 6.

3
DRESSINGS,
SAUCES
AND GRAVIES

Thickening agents, readily available through supermarkets and health-food stores are: cornflour (make sure it's pure corn only), arrowroot, potato flour, wholewheat flour, brown-rice flour and rice bran polishings. Cornflour and arrowroot produce velvety-textured mixtures with very little flavour, as does potato flour. They are particularly suited to thickening sweet sauces and Chinese-style dishes and casseroles. A word of caution: the same amount of arrowroot produces a much thicker and rather elastic (some say "rubbery") consistency compared with cornflour, so reduce the quantity of arrowroot used when substituting for cornflour.

Wholewheat flour, brown-rice flour and rice bran produce less finely textured mixtures and are particularly good for thickening gravies, casseroles and savoury dressings. Another word of caution: brown-rice flour is slower to act than is wholewheat flour, but will produce just as thick a consistency given extra time. If extra rice flour is added, a very stiff mixture will result. Rice bran, unlike wheat bran, goes smooth and pasty when liquid is added—excellent for gravies.

Substitute with whatever is tolerated, bearing in mind the above cautions and guidelines. I think I would have to draw the line at using rice bran in custard, for instance. I know of no-one allergic to arrowroot, so hopefully all of you with food allergies will have at least one thickener available, and a versatile one at that, to use in the following recipes.

Excess amounts may be frozen in small quantities.

Boiled Salad Dressing

    1 tablespoon plain flour (wholewheat, brown-rice flour, potato flour or arrowroot)
    ½ teaspoon mustard powder
    ¼ teaspoon ground black pepper
    1 teaspoon fructose (optional)
    1 cup goat's or soya milk
    juice ½ lemon (or to taste)
    15 g (½ oz) margarine

Mix together the dry ingredients. Add the milk, stirring constantly, then gradually blend in the lemon juice, adjusting the quantity to taste. Melt the margarine in a saucepan and add the blended mixture; beat until thoroughly mixed. Boil gently for three minutes. Cool, and freeze excess in serving-size portions. Makes 1¼ cups.

Basic White Sauce

    1 tablespoon margarine
    1 tablespoon wheat flour or 1 dessertspoon arrowroot, brown-rice flour, potato flour or cornflour
    1 cup goat's or soya milk
    desired seasonings

Melt margarine in a small pan, then add flour and cook, stirring constantly, for one minute. Remove pan from heat. Gradually add ½ cup milk, stirring well until smooth. Return pan to heat and add remaining milk; stir till thickened and season to taste. If a very thick white sauce is needed for savoury fillings, increase amounts of margarine and flour.

Cauliflower Sauce

To the Basic White Sauce add either or both of these: finely chopped fresh parsley—1 dessertspoon or more; ½ cup cooked mashed pumpkin. These produce a colourful sauce.

Italian-style Tomato Sauce

See recipe p. 33.

Sweet 'n' Spicy Tomato Sauce

1 tablespoon oil
1 chopped onion
500 g (1 lb) peeled and chopped tomatoes
1 tablespoon pure tomato paste (optional)
1 peeled and sliced apple
1 chopped stick celery or celery tops
¼ teaspoon ground pimento (allspice)
½ cup water
½ teaspoon kelp powder (optional)
black pepper to taste

Heat oil in a saucepan, then sauté onion until golden. Add remaining ingredients, and simmer covered, for 25 minutes, removing lid for the final minutes if the mixture is too runny. Purée or process in an electric blender or food processor and freeze any excess. Serve warm or cold as an accompaniment to meat or egg dishes or in pizzas (see p. 32). This sauce is more like the commercial bottled tomato sauce.

Gravy

Simply substitute appropriately when dredging meat before browning, or when making basic gravy in the usual way. It is easier to make lump-free gravy with brown-rice flour or rice bran than with wheat flour. Before you add more flour, remember that rice flour takes longer to thicken. Any of the thickeners given at the start of this chapter may be used for gravy. The natural brown colour of rice bran produces a rich-coloured gravy.

Boiled Custard

2 cups goat's milk
1 beaten egg
4 teaspoons arrowroot or 1½ tablespoons potato flour
3 teaspoons fructose or honey to taste or liquefy ¼ cup sultanas
    first in some of the milk
vanilla essence (optional)

Heat the milk till almost boiling. Add vanilla if used. Beat the egg with arrowroot and fructose, and add this mixture to the hot milk; stir well until the mixture thickens, then allow to boil gently for one minute. Remove from the heat—the custard will firm further as it cools. Adjust the amount of arrowroot depending on whether you want a pouring custard or a thicker one. Add extra arrowroot cautiously, as the custard quickly becomes very rubbery.

Honey Caramel Sauce

1 well-rounded tablespoon margarine
1½ level teaspoons fructose
2 tablespoons goat's or soya milk
2 dessertspoons honey
2 rounded dessertspoons arrowroot
2 tablespoons hot water

Melt the margarine in a saucepan, then add the other ingredients except the hot water. Stir well over the heat until the mixture is smooth and has thickened. Remove from heat and add the hot water gradually, beating well until it is smooth. Use immediately as a pouring sauce, or chill if a firm spread is required. Store in a jar in the refrigerator. Makes ½ cup.

Cherry "Cranberry" Sauce

250 g (8 oz) fresh cherries, pitted and finely chopped or puréed
¾ cup water
3 teaspoons fructose
1 teaspoon gelatine softened in 1 dessertspoon cold water

Add all ingredients to a saucepan and bring to the boil. Simmer only until the fructose is dissolved, and the colour has changed from cherry to brownish. Then refrigerate till the mixture is firm. The sauce may also be frozen.

Chocolate-type Carob Sauce (sweetener-free)

125 g (4 oz) copha
4 teaspoons margarine
8 tablespoons carob powder

Melt the copha. Add the margarine and stir till melted and well blended. Do not boil or overheat. Remove from heat and stir in the carob powder; beat till smooth. Use immediately for a pouring sauce or leave to cool and thicken. Makes about 1⅓ cups of sauce.

Note: If replacing the carob with cocoa you may want to add some sweetener, for example, fructose or Equal; sweeteners should be mixed in, off the heat, after the cocoa has been added. See also Carob-coated Nuts 'n' Raisins, p. 203, and Sundaes, p. 175.

4
SALADS

Most people with multiple food allergies still have a wide range of vegetables to choose from—either to cook or eat fresh in salads. I have been amazed at the range of vegetables my children will eat if given the chance to try the vegetables completely undressed and frequently raw or only lightly steamed. For example, my children love fresh beetroot steamed till tender. I hated beetroot until I discovered that what I hated was the vinegar dressing not the beetroot. A little white vinegar is allowed for those allergic to yeast, since white vinegar is made from acetic acid.

The recipes that follow offer a few variations on old themes and ways of coping with restricted dressings.

Fruity Coleslaw (vinegar-free)

>   2 cups finely sliced cabbage
>   1 cup grated carrot
>   ½ cup finely sliced or chopped celery
>   1 cup apple, washed, cored and diced (retain skin for colour)
>   1 tablespoon coarsley chopped walnuts

Mix all the ingredients together. Toss in ¼-½ cup of any of the following with ½ teaspoon vitamin C powder added to help prevent any browning of the vegetables—orange juice, freshly squeezed; pineapple juice, unsweetened tinned or freshly squeezed; apple juice, unsweetened tinned or freshly squeezed; or, if a mayonnaise effect is required, toss in 1 tablespoon or more of Boiled Salad Dressing (recipe p. 44), chilled and thinned down if necessary with extra goat's milk.

   Always stir coleslaw immediately before serving to mix the developed juices through evenly. Serves 4-6.

Winter Salad

>   ½ cup fresh beetroot, steamed then diced
>   ½ cup finely sliced celery
>   ½ cup peeled and diced apple
>   1 dessertspoon chopped walnuts

Mix all ingredients together thoroughly, then add your choice of: 1 dessertspoon goat's yoghurt, or 1 tablespoon goat's cottage cheese (or tofu) plain, or creamed with a little lemon juice, or 1 dessertspoon Boiled Salad Dressing (recipe p. 44). Toss well, then chill before serving. This salad has a striking pink colour. Serves 4.

Carrot Salad

To the desired amount of grated carrot add raisins and/or unsulphured dried apricots, both of which have been previously steeped for a few minutes in boiling water. Toss the salad in orange juice, or water with ½ teaspoon of vitamin C powder added, to prevent the carrot turning brown. Alternatively, coat the salad in any of the suggestions given under Winter Salad.

Moulded Salad

1½ tablespoons gelatine
½ cup cold water
1 cup boiling water
1 tablespoon lemon juice
½ cup fresh apple juice or tinned unsweetened pineapple juice
¼ teaspoon vitamin C powder
1 cup sliced banana
½ cup cooked green peas
½ cup canned unsweetened pineapple pieces
½ cup grated raw apple

Soak the gelatine in the cold water, then add the boiling water and stir until the gelatine is dissolved. Add the lemon juice and fruit juice and allow to cool. As soon as the jelly begins to thicken, fold in the remaining ingredients. Pour the jelly into a wetted five-cup mould and chill until firm. Turn out onto a plate lined with the whole leaves of a green, leafy vegetable, such as lettuce, cabbage or spinach. Decorate with red pepper slices and parsley sprigs.

The faintly lemon-flavoured jelly in this recipe may form the basis of different moulded salads. Remember that fresh pineapple digests protein, such as gelatine, so only canned (unsweetened) pineapple can be used in gelatine recipes. When omitting the sugar often present in moulded salad recipes, decrease the lemon juice and add fruit juice to make up the volume and add natural sweetness.

Undressed Fresh Salads

If the above recipes do not suit you, and for whatever reason you are unable to have any of the dressings suggested above,

Sweet Sausages

*700 g (1½ lb) lean pork, beef or veal or any combination (using
   more pork than beef and veal)*
125-200 g (4-6 oz) pork fat
½ medium finely grated onion
4 teaspoons dried basil leaves
1 tablespoon chopped parsley
⅛ teaspoon pepper
½ teaspoon nutmeg
¼ teaspoon ground thyme

Chop the meat and fat, mix together and mince or process in a
food processor briefly. Add the remaining ingredients and
knead thoroughly; shape with wet hands. Chill the sausages
until required, or freeze. They may be simmered gently in
homemade tomato sauce, grilled or barbecued.

Stuffings

Basic Herb Stuffing

125-200 g (4-6 oz) margarine
1 finely chopped onion
4 cups breadcrumbs
½ cup finely chopped parsley
black pepper to taste
herbs, for example, tarragon, thyme, marjoram, sage

Melt the margarine, add onion and cook gently until onion is
transparent. Combine with remaining ingredients and mix
well. Add more melted margarine if the mixture is too dry. The
stuffing may be used to stuff red meat, such as boned breast or
leg of lamb, or roast poultry.

Use any allowable bread (see recipes in Chapter 7). Rolled
oats and cooked rice are other substitutes for the breadcrumbs,
but adjust the margarine in proportion.

A tasty addition to the basic mixture is one lamb's kidney

cored and finely chopped—use to stuff a boned shoulder of lamb. Other meats may also be added to the basic mixture, for example, pork and veal mince for turkey stuffing, and bacon if tolerated. You may prefer to omit the herbs when meats are used and perhaps include some chopped celery.

Other interesting stuffings are: cherry-cheese stuffing with muesli (see recipe p. 190); and roasted loin or boned leg of lamb with herb stuffing and fruit topping (recipe follows):

Herb Stuffing and Fruit Topping for Lamb

Stuffing
>   1 chopped onion
>   ½ cup finely chopped parsley
>   good pinch dried thyme
>   1 teaspoon dried tarragon leaves
>   pepper to taste
>   1 tablespoon natural yoghurt
>   4 tablespoons or more rice bran

Mix all ingredients together well or process briefly in a food processor. Adjust yoghurt and bran quantities, if necessary, to achieve the correct stuffing consistency. Stuff into a cavity of boned leg and tie up well, or pack between chops of loin roast, tying up loin securely. Bake as normal and coat meat with the topping for the final 30 minutes.

Topping
>   1 cup chopped fresh or dried apple and apricots
>   1 tablespoon margarine
>   rice bran
>   sage (optional)

Mix the ingredients together, adding sufficient rice bran to make a mixture thick enough to coat the meat. Return the meat to the oven to complete cooking and to soften and brown the topping.

Apple- and Cheese-stuffed Pork Chops

4 large pork chops (cut horizontally to form a pocket)

Stuffing

    1 large apple
    250 g (8 oz) goat's cottage cheese or tofu
    2-3 tablespoons fresh breadcrumbs or cooked rice
    1 teaspoon sage
    pepper to taste

Sauce

    2 large apples, peeled, cored and cut into rings
    margarine for frying
    1 large sliced onion
    450 ml (¾ pint) fresh or unsweetened tinned apple juice
    1 tablespoon chopped parsley
    arrowroot for thickening

To make the stuffing, coarsely grate the peeled apple and mix all stuffing ingredients together evenly. Fill the pockets of chops with the stuffing and fasten with skewers or string. To cook the chops, fry the apple rings in margarine until golden; remove from pan. Add chops and brown quickly on both sides. Add sliced onion, apple juice and any ends of the chopped apple. Cover and simmer gently for 20 minutes or until cooked, turning chops once during cooking. To serve, remove meat to a serving dish, garnish with the warm apple rings and pour over the sauce, thickened if necessary with a little arrowroot, adding ½ cup of water. Garnish with parsley.

Spinach Stuffing for Roast Poultry

50 g (2 oz) margarine
½ cup finely chopped onion
250 g (8 oz) fresh spinach or 125 g (4 oz) silver beet
3 tablespoons soft breadcrumbs
grated rind ½ lemon
1 egg (optional)
250 g (8 oz) goat's cottage cheese or soya tofu
1 tablespoon finely chopped chives

Melt 25 g (1 oz) of the margarine, add the onion and cook until softened. Wash the spinach or silver beet thoroughly, discard the stalks and chop the leaves coarsely; add to the onion and cook both gently for 10 minutes or until the spinach is soft. Remove from heat and stir in the breadcrumbs, rind, egg (if used), chives and cheese. Allow to cool before stuffing the chicken.

This recipe makes sufficient stuffing for a large roasting chicken of about 1½-2 kg (3-4 lb).

6
BREAKFAST GRAINS

I was brought up with the idea that breakfast was an important, not-to-be-missed meal of the day, and I still firmly believe in the energy value to be gained from a good breakfast. Allergies to grains are common, and may be to more than one grain. Most of the prepared commercial cereals are wheat-based, most have added sugar, honey and salt even if they are wholegrain, which most are not, and then those which are free from these things are most likely a "healthy" mixture of several grains, which can be most unhealthy if you happen to be allergic to even one of them.

So how do you go about starting this good breakfast? If you can tolerate wheat and/or rice, then there are shredded wheat and puffed wholewheat cereals, and wholegrain (brown) puffed rice cereals without additives, available from health-food stores and some supermarkets. Improve the nutrition content by adding your choice of nuts and seeds, dried and fresh fruit in season, milk and/or yoghurt/soya milk/fruit juice. If you can tolerate oats, then the ordinary (not the instant) rolled oats can be used in your own favourite muesli recipe or to make porridge. Rolled forms of wheat, barley, rye, rice and millet are also available, providing a good choice of grains to substitute or rotate when making your own prepared cereal.

There follows a basic muesli recipe, which our family used for some time, and I then show the changes made when wheat and oats became allergy foods for us.

Mixed-grain Muesli

½ cup oil (sunflower, safflower or whatever is tolerated)
1½ teaspoons pure vanilla essence (or to taste)
¼ cup sesame seeds
½ cup chopped unblanched almonds
¼ cup soya nuts (soya beans cooked and roasted) (optional)
1 cup coconut
½ cup wheatgerm (optional)
3½ cups rolled oats

In a large saucepan, heat the oil gently, add vanilla and stir until it is mixed through. Remove pan from stove, and add remaining ingredients gradually in the order listed, stirring well between additions. Store muesli in airtight containers or make toasted muesli by spreading the prepared muesli on large oven trays and placing in a 180°C (350°F) oven. Once the muesli begins to colour (25 minutes or so), stir carefully every 10 minutes to prevent scorching around the edges. Toast according to your preference. Cool and store in airtight containers. When serving, add fresh fruit, chopped or lightly stewed (my children's favourite is grated apple), or dried fruit if tolerated, and milk (goat's or soya) or fruit juice. A wheat-free variation could be made by omitting wheatgerm and substituting an equal quantity of rice bran (polishings); an oat-free one by omitting rolled oats and substituting the rolled or flaked version of any other tolerated grain.

Whole-rice Muesli

½ cup oil (or less if preferred)
1 teaspoon pure vanilla essence (optional)
¼ cup sesame seeds (optional)
½ cup chopped almonds
1 cup coconut
1½ cups rice bran
3½ cups rolled rice (rice flakes)

Heat the oil gently in a large saucepan, add vanilla and stir until it is mixed through. Remove pan from heat, and add remaining ingredients gradually in the order listed, stirring well between additions. If the vanilla is omitted, then the oil does not have to be heated and the recipe becomes very simple to make. It is a more "dressed-up" mixture than eating the plain rolled grain and is used in the popular whole-rice White Christmas recipe (p. 185) and Lincoln Crisps (p. 119), as well as being an ingredient in a stuffing for roast duck (p. 190). This basic recipe also lends itself well to being used in a rotary diet; simply proceed with the recipe up to the bran and rolled rice, then, perhaps using these rice grains for one of them, make up four or five different mueslis using 5 cups each time of the grain chosen for each muesli. Some of the rolled grain ground to a finer flour in a food processor or electric blender could be used to replace the 1½ cups of rice bran in order to keep the grain constant in the one muesli. Store each muesli in well-labelled containers.

Porridge

Substitute pure rolled versions of another grain if oats are not tolerated. Make the recipe as usual, using goat's milk, a combination of goat's milk and water, soya milk, or simply water. Try adding a sprinkling of any dried fruit during the cooking to help replace the sweetness you may have been used to when dark-brown sugar was an accompaniment to the porridge. A dash of cinnamon, stirred in well during the cooking, will add a spice treat. Finally, top the cooked porridge with any fresh fruit, such as raw banana or grated apple, or any lightly stewed stone fruit.

Cinnamon Muesli

2 cups sultanas
water
1 teaspoon cinnamon (or to taste)
18 cups (or less as preferred) rolled oats or other rolled grain

Place the sultanas in a saucepan with water to cover; add the cinnamon and simmer until the water is evaporated, taking care that the pan does not scorch. Add 4 cups of oats and mix well. Remove pan from the stove and process the mixture in a blender or food processor until it is finely chopped. Rub this mixture into the remaining oats. Chopped nuts and/or seeds may be added. Store in airtight containers and use as cold muesli or in your porridge recipe, or even as a fruit crumble topping.

For other breakfast cereal ideas, cooked or uncooked, consult American cookery books in particular as breakfast is a more important meal in America than here. I recommend especially: *Diet for a Small Planet* by F. M. Lappe, Ballantine Books, 1978, and its companion: *Recipes for a Small Planet* by E. B. Ewald, Ballantine Books, 1978. These books certainly tell you how to make the most nutritious of breakfast options.

7
BREAD
AND
ROLLS

Bread is undoubtedly a staple food in the average Australian's diet. In this chapter there are many variations on the basic recipe, so that there is a possible recipe no matter what your grain allergy is.

All the bread recipes are yeast-free. They are essentially soda breads, with bicarbonate of soda being the rising agent rather than baker's yeast. Soured milk is traditionally included in soda bread with the bicarbonate of soda, but the following recipes include cream of tartar to balance and facilitate the action of the bicarbonate of soda for those who prefer not to, or cannot, use the lemon juice added to sour the milk. If you can, use the lemon juice, or at least some of it, as well, to ensure neutrality of the baked product (see "Ingredients": "Bicarbonate of Soda", p. 13) and for a more savoury taste.

Soda breads are mixed like a scone dough, with no kneading process, so they are much quicker to make than yeast breads. Soda breads do not keep well so either bake one loaf at a time, or else slice and freeze the extra loaves as soon as they have cooled. The frozen slices separate easily and thus are available for toast and for sandwich-making—using frozen slices for sandwiches, particularly in summer, ensures that any salad filling is still cold and fresh by the time the lunch-hour comes, but the bread has had time to thaw.

The shape of the loaf is up to you—the mixture can be

shaped into the traditional soda bread round, placed on a flat oven tray and a deep cross can be slashed on the top. If it is a sandwich loaf you need, then spoon the mixture into a loaf tin. For rolls, use the same mixture, but simply spoon heaped tablespoons of it close together in baking pans which have at least a small side to them to contain the mixture.

To make any soda bread loaf you will need:

6 cups flour or mixture of flours
1½ teaspoons bicarbonate of soda (rising agent)
3 teaspoons cream of tartar (acts with soda and balances it)
3 cups or more liquid (see list of options following)
1 tablespoon lemon juice (also balances the soda; optional)

I use no salt for nutritional reasons and because my family has adjusted gradually to omitting salt. It may, of course, be added if you prefer, or you may use one of the low-sodium "salts" on the market, but check labels for other ingredients.

This makes a large loaf, 27 by 11 cm (10 by 4 in), particularly if using wholewheat flour which rises more than the other flours. For a smaller loaf tin, 22 by 11 cm (9 by 4 in), use:

4 cups flour
1¼ teaspoons bicarbonate of soda
2½ teaspoons cream of tartar
about 2½ cups liquid (depending on flour used)

The basic method involves adding the lemon juice to the milk (if used), and allowing it to stand while the flour is prepared. If no milk is used, simply add the lemon juice (if used) to the other liquid. Sift 3 or 4 cups of the flour with the other dry ingredients then add to the rest of the flour in a large bowl. Make a well in the centre of the flour and add the liquids; mix thoroughly to form a dough. Bake as directed in the recipe, usually in a tin lined with greased and floured greaseproof or brown paper, and bake for 1½ hours or so in a moderate oven. Cover the top of the loaf with greaseproof or aluminium foil to prevent the crust becoming too hard before the centre of the loaf is cooked. A hard crust makes slicing difficult since the non-wheat soda breads tend to be more fragile anyway. Gentle slicing is needed, perhaps with the loaf upside down so that you start cutting through the smooth under-surface rather than the rougher crust. An electric knife is often useful, particularly with the heavier grains, such as rye and oats.

When devising your own recipe, keep the above proportions in mind. There is nothing magical about the following bread recipes, so do experiment yourself until you find a balance you like. The quantities are a guide only and may be varied substantially without spoiling the end result. Soda bread is not tricky to make.

Each of the flours has different taste and baking qualities which add to the fun of experimenting with them. Here are some guidelines to help you on your way.

Wholewheat

This flour can be bought as the coarser baker's meal or finer 100 per cent wholewheat flour. It gives a heavier but definitely more substantial and flavoursome result compared to white flour. It still handles easily in baking and will develop a good degree of elasticity where this is desirable, for example, in pastries, pasta and bread. Be aware that most of the flour in supermarkets labelled wholemeal flour is only 50 per cent wholewheat and 50 per cent plain white flour.

Oats

Oatmeal flour may be purchased from health-food stores. I prefer simply to grind my own from the simple rolled oats using an electric blender or food processor. Oat flour produces a heavy coarse-textured bread without a strong taste. A few unground rolled oats tossed in produces an interesting nutty texture and helps break up the otherwise rather stodgy consistency. Oat flour combines well with flours which on their own would produce a smoother, finer texture, such as rye or soya flour.

Corn

Corn or maizemeal is available coarsely or finely ground. As cornmeal is low in gluten, the final baked product is often crumbly, so eggs, milk, margarine and/or combining the cornmeal with another more sticky flour, such as rye or soya, is desirable. Rolls or muffins may be easier to handle than loaves which require thin slicing. When using cornmeal, one method is to heat the liquid specified to boiling, then pour it over the cornmeal. Mix and let it stand briefly before adding the other ingredients. When buying the thickener cornflour, be sure to get pure maize flour as sometimes there is some other grain, such as wheat, added.

Rye

A traditionally dark flour with a characteristic strong flavour, it produces a fine-textured loaf, though heavy. It has sufficient gluten to develop some pliability when used on its own, and it has very different cooking characteristics compared to the other common flours. If a loaf containing predominantly rye flour was cooked in the usual manner, it would have a crust so hard that even an electric knife would have trouble cutting through, yet the centre would be uncooked. Two alternative ways of coping with rye-flour loaves are:

• Bake the loaf for several hours in a slow oven, but with the loaf tin covered with foil and set in a water bath. Remove foil to brown the top for last 30 minutes to one hour of cooking, when most of the water should have evaporated.
• Use a microwave oven if you have one. A two-hour cooking time can be shortened to 20 minutes, though beware of substantial shrinkage if the heat is too high.

Rye-flour rolls do not require such special cooking procedures (see "Rolls", p. 84).

Soya Flour

A yellowish flour, low in gluten, producing a fine but quite close-textured loaf. Most people find soya flour, particularly the full-fat flour, unpalatable on its own, but it combines well with other flours, such as oat, rice or cornflour, and only a small amount of another flour makes a big taste difference. Make sure a soya-flour loaf is completely cooked—uncooked soya dough has a strong taste. Soya flour is available with various amounts of fat left in, and as the fat contains lecithin, this is good nutritionally. The recipes in this book assume the use of full-fat soya flour unless otherwise stated. De-fatted soya flour has a milder taste but is more difficult to handle than the full-fat flour. Soya flour is an excellent high-protein addition to other flours.

Buckwheat

This flour is not a member of the grain family, but is in the same family as rhubarb. Despite this being useful to those following the rotary diet approach to coping with food allergies, any rhubarb-hater may say that it is obvious from the taste. Buckwheat is a greyish flour with a very strong and unique flavour, so it is best combined with other flours. Fruit buns or raisin bread with lots of spice added produces a more palatable result.

Rice

A very versatile flour, used only in its wholegrain or brown form in this book. In baking, I often use a combination of brown-rice flour and rice bran or polishings rather than brown rice flour on its own. Unlike wholewheat bran, rice bran is not obviously fibrous—when liquid is added it goes pasty and smooth and produces a more cakey texture than does brown-rice flour, which left to itself produces a rather more gritty or "sandy" product and one which tends to crumble. The good news about rice bran it that it is freely available from health-food stores and is very cheap.

Yes, it *is* possible to make breads (and cakes and biscuits even more so, see Chapters 10 and 11) using only the rice flours. Make sure ample liquid is used and that the mixture is beaten thoroughly for a smoother product.

Millet

Less commonly used, millet has a quite strong taste.

Triticale Flour

A true hybrid of wheat and rye in all its qualities. Check for tolerance if you are allergic to either grain.

Potato Flour

A useful addition to other flours to give a smoother, finer texture. It is more suited to cakes and biscuits than to bread-making if used on its own. It is an excellent thickener (see Chapter 3) and produces a very smooth-textured sauce.

Arrowroot

This is also a useful addition as a smooth, dry, binding flour, but not as a bread flour on its own.

Semolina

This flour is a form of wheat; it is milled from hard durum wheat, and is higher in protein and gluten than the other wheat strains. However, it is not suitable for those allergic to wheat.

Liquids

The *liquid options* are: water, or goat's milk, or goat's milk and water (which produces a lighter product than pure goat's milk), or soya milk, or soya milk and water mixed (if powdered milk is used, add powder with dry ingredients and add water as the liquid); or vegetable stock, or chicken stock skimmed of fat to make a more savoury loaf, or fruit juice (if making raisin bread). The amount of liquid will depend to a degree on the batch of flour being used, so adjust where necessary. A word of reassurance here is that low-gluten flours, such as soya, buckwheat and corn, can be a problem when trying to be exact about amounts of liquid and baking time. Even when you have measured precisely, do be prepared to adjust either or both for any particular loaf you make—a sizeable leeway is permitted. Once you have a feel for soda bread, you will probably be better off not relying on precise measurements.

Some of the breads tend to be sticky even when cooked. They can benefit by being simply wrapped in a towel and left to dry out overnight and cool thoroughly. These loaves are also best kept in the refrigerator and are often even easier to slice when chilled.

Armed, now, with this information about the basic recipe and the different characteristics of the flour and liquid ingredients, you are ready to start putting together a loaf that meets your particular needs. Alternatively, start off with one or more of the recipes given below.

Amongst the yeast-free breads available commercially, there are rye-only, wheat-only and multi-grain varieties. Read the labels very carefully as identical-looking breads may have slightly different ingredients. A few are also milk-, sugar- and honey-free. Such specialist breads, available chiefly through health-food stores, are most likely free from artificial additives such as preservatives, but do check this with the storekeeper.

Wholewheat Soda Bread

1 tablespoon lemon juice
3 cups goat's milk or milk and water mixed or other tolerated
   liquid (see options above)
6 cups 100 per cent wholewheat flour (preferably stoneground)
1½ teaspoons bicarbonate of soda
3 teaspoons cream of tartar
1 teaspoon kelp powder (optional)
sesame seeds (optional)

Mix the lemon juice with 2 cups of the milk and leave to stand
while preparing flour. Place 4 cups of the flour in a large
mixing bowl. Sift in remaining 2 cups of flour with soda, cream
of tartar and kelp. Make a well in the centre of the flour and
pour in the liquid and lemon juice; mix thoroughly but lightly.
If making a round loaf, the consistency should hold its own
shape. If using a loaf tin or making rolls, the consistency may
be softer, so adjust the liquid amounts accordingly. Again, a fair
degree of variation is possible here.

Either shape the mixture into a round and place on a
greased and floured oven tray, or line the bottom of a large loaf
tin with greaseproof or brown paper greased with oil or
dripping and then lightly floured. Spoon the mixture into the
tin, brush the top with milk or melted margarine or water and
sprinkle with sesame seeds, if liked. Bake in a preheated oven at
190°C (375°F) for about 50 minutes (less if in a round) or until
risen, browned and with the sides just shrinking away from the
tin. Turn loaf out of the tin, wrap it in a clean teatowel and
leave to cool completely before cutting. Variations on this
recipe are to add ½ cup sesame seeds to the mixture; or add ¾
cup dried fruit—sultanas and/or currants and/or chopped
raisins—and 1 teaspoon each of cinnamon and mixed spice (or
more to taste) for a delicious wholemeal raisin bread. The liquid
in this case could be fruit juice, such as apple, orange, pineapple
or pear.

Lebanese Wholewheat Pocket Bread

1 kg (2 lb) wholemeal flour
3 teaspoons bicarbonate of soda
6 teaspoons cream of tartar
1 teaspoon kelp powder (optional)
4 cups warm water or vegetable stock

Sift some of the flour with the soda, cream of tartar and kelp. Add the liquid to the dry ingredients and knead the dough, using more flour if necessary, until smooth and elastic. Cover the dough loosely with plastic food wrap (the dough will expand a little) and leave for at least three hours or overnight.

Take portions of the dough and roll them into flat rounds. Cook on oven racks in a very hot oven at 230°-250°C (450°-475°F) for about 10 minutes, or until puffed and cooked. Slit with a sharp knife while still hot if a "pocket" is desired.

Rye-oat Soda Bread

2 tablespoons lemon juice (optional)
7 cups liquid (see "Liquids", p. 75)
6½ cups rye flour
2 teaspoons kelp powder (optional)
3 teaspoons bicarbonate of soda
6 teaspoons cream of tartar
4 cups ground oat flour or oatmeal
1½ cups rolled oats

Mix the lemon juice with 1 cup of milk (if used), and set aside. Sift together 4 cups of rye flour with the kelp, soda and cream of tartar. Add these to a large bowl with the rest of the flours and rolled oats. Make a well in the centre of the flour and pour in half the liquid ingredients. Mix well, then add remaining liquid, mixing thoroughly again. Spoon the dough into greased loaf tins, lined on the bottom and sides with greased and floured greaseproof or brown paper—tins should be a good three-quarters or more full. Place loaves in a larger container filled with hot water to reach halfway up the sides of the tins; then cover loaves loosely (to allow for rising) with foil.

Place in an oven preheated to 160°C (325°F) and bake for two hours. Remove foil and bake a further one hour—the water will gradually evaporate during cooking. Wrap cooked loaves in a clean teatowel and cool completely before slicing. Makes two large loaves.

Rye-soya Soda Bread

1 tablespoon lemon juice (optional)
3 cups liquid (see "Liquids", p. 75)
4 cups rye flour
1 teaspoon kelp powder (optional)
1½ teaspoons bicarbonate of soda
3 teaspoons cream of tartar
2 cups soya flour

Mix the lemon juice with 1 cup of milk (if used), and set aside. Sift together 3 cups of rye flour with the kelp, soda and cream of tartar. Add these with the remaining flours to a large bowl. Make a well in the centre of the flour and pour in half the liquid ingredients. Mix well, then add remaining liquid, mixing thoroughly again. Spoon the dough into a greased loaf tin lined on the bottom and sides with greased and floured greaseproof or brown paper—the tin should be a good three-quarters full. Place tin in a larger container filled with hot water to reach halfway up the sides of the tin; then cover loaf loosely with foil.

Place in a preheated oven at 160°C (325°F) and bake for two hours. Remove foil and bake for a further hour—the water will evaporate during cooking. Wrap loaf in a clean teatowel and cool completely before slicing. Makes one large loaf.

Rye-rice Soda Bread

1-2 tablespoons lemon juice (to taste) (optional)
7½ cups liquid (see "Liquids", p. 75)
6 cups rye flour
3 teaspoons bicarbonate of soda
6 teaspoons cream of tartar
4 cups brown-rice flour
2 cups rice bran

Mix the lemon juice with 1 cup of milk (if used), and set aside. Sift together 4 cups of rye flour with the soda and cream of tartar. Add these with the remaining flours and the rice bran to a large bowl. Make a well in the centre of the flour and pour in the liquid ingredients. Mix well, then add remaining liquid, mixing thoroughly. Spoon the dough into greased loaf tins, lined on the bottom and sides with greased and floured grease-proof or brown paper—the tins should be three-quarters or more full. Place loaves in a larger container filled with hot water to reach halfway up the sides of the tins; then cover loaves loosely with foil.

Place in a preheated oven at 160°C (325°F) and bake for two hours. Remove foil and bake for a further hour—the water will evaporate during cooking. Wrap loaves in a clean teatowel and allow to cool before slicing. Makes two large or three small loaves.

Soya-oat Soda Bread

1 tablespoon lemon juice (optional)
3 cups liquid (soya milk would be in keeping with the soya flour)
2½ cups soya flour
2½ cups ground oat flour
1 cup rolled oats
1 teaspoon kelp powder (optional)
1½ teaspoons bicarbonate of soda
3 teaspoons cream of tartar

Mix the lemon juice with the milk (if used), and set aside. Sift the flours with the other dry ingredients. Make a well in the centre of the flour, add the liquid ingredients and mix thoroughly and quickly to form a dough. Spoon the mixture into a greased loaf tin, lined on the bottom and sides with greased and floured greaseproof or brown paper. No waterbath is needed, so simply place the loaf in an oven preheated to 180°C (350°F) and bake for 1½-2 hours or until golden. Remove from tin, wrap in a clean teatowel and leave to cool before slicing.

This recipe also makes delicious rolls or muffins for entertaining, barbecues, etcetera. I have found them popular with people who know nothing of food allergies. Makes one large loaf.

Soya, Rice and Potato Bread

1 tablespoon lemon juice (optional)
3 cups liquid (see "Liquids", p. 75)
3 cups soya flour
1 teaspoon kelp powder (optional)
1½ teaspoons bicarbonate of soda
3 teaspoons cream of tartar
1½ cups brown-rice flour
1½ cups potato flour

Mix the lemon juice with the milk (if used), and set aside. Sift 2 cups of soya flour with all the remaining dry ingredients except the rice flour and the oats, then add to a large bowl with the remaining flours and oats, mixing well. Make a well in the centre of the flour, add the liquid ingredients and mix thoroughly. Spoon the mixture into a greased loaf tin, lined on the bottom and sides with greased and floured greaseproof or brown paper. No waterbath is needed, so simply bake loaf in a preheated oven at 180°C (350°F) for 1½-2 hours or until golden. Remove from tin, wrap in a clean teatowel and leave to cool before slicing. Makes one large loaf.

Barley, Rice and Potato Bread

about 2½ cups half milk (goat's or soya), half water
1 tablespoon lemon juice (optional)
3 cups barley flour
1 cup rice flour
1 teaspoon bicarbonate of soda
2 teaspoons cream of tartar
1 small boiled potato

Mix a little milk with the lemon juice (if used), and set aside. Sift all dry ingredients together. Rub in cold mashed potato, add milk and water and mix to a soft smooth dough quickly. Turn the dough into a greased loaf tin (it should be about full), smooth the top with a knife dipped in melted margarine and bake for 45-50 minutes in a hot oven at 200°C (400°F). Remove from the tin and cool on a rack wrapped in a teatowel. Makes one small loaf.

Soya-rice Combinations

When using a good proportion of rice flour and rice bran I have found that the texture of the loaf and its pliability are greatly improved if the mixture is well beaten once the liquid has been added.

Experiment with proportions of soya and rice flours. A general proportion I have found pleasing is equal or greater total rice (flour and/or bran) than soya flour. The consistency should be fairly stiff for ease of baking right through the loaf, so do not add too much liquid though the dough is better if softer for rolls.

Examples of two variations are:

Soya-rice Flour Bread

2 cups soya flour   }   or   { 2 cups soya flour
2 cups brown-rice flour   1 cup brown-rice flour
                                    1 cup rice bran
1 tablespoon lemon juice (optional)
3 cups liquid (see "Liquids", p. 75)
1 teaspoon bicarbonate of soda
2 teaspoons cream of tartar

Mix the lemon juice with the milk (if used), and set aside. Sift 1 cup of soya flour with the soda and cream of tartar. Then add to a large bowl with the other flours (and the bran in the second variation), make a well in the centre and add the liquid ingredients; mix thoroughly to form a dough. Spoon the dough into greased loaf tins, lined with greased and floured grease-proof or brown paper. Bake in a preheated oven at 180°C (350°F) for 1½-2 hours or until golden. Remove from tin, wrap in a clean teatowel and allow to cool before slicing. Makes one small loaf.

To show further how proportions of grains may be changed easily, compare the following three recipes:

Three-grain Loaf

3½ cups soya flour } or { 2 cups soya flour } or { 1½ cups soya flour
2 cups buck-wheat flour   2 cups buck-wheat flour   2 cups buck-wheat flour
½ cup rice bran   2 cups rice bran   2 cups rice bran
                                                           ½ cup brown-rice flour

For remaining ingredients and method and baking, see Soya-oat Soda Bread, p. 79. Try them out. Which do you prefer?

Five-grain Loaf

    1 cup barley flour
    1 cup brown-rice flour
    1 cup soya flour
    1 cup fine cornmeal
    1 teaspoon bicarbonate of soda
    2 teaspoons cream of tartar
    1 small boiled mashed potato
    2½-3 cups half milk (goat's or soya) and half water

Sift all the dry ingredients together. Rub in the cold mashed potato, and milk and water, and mix to a soft smooth dough quickly. Turn the dough into a greased loaf tin (it should be about full), smooth the top with a knife dipped in melted margarine and bake for 45-50 minutes in a hot oven at 200°C (400°F). Remove loaf from the tin and cool on a rack wrapped in a teatowel. (Grease and line the tin well since cornmeal tends to stick.) Makes one small loaf.

Rice Bread or Rolls

The first of the following recipes, while not wholly rice, is nearly so and holds together more easily than the second recipe. The first may be made into a small loaf, in which case double the quantity to 4 cups of flour. Both recipes take well to being made into rolls—the best solution to a bread that tends to crumble. The addition of an egg, if tolerated, would help bind the mixture—this is why the margarine is included in the second recipe. The arrowroot flour binds the first mixture well. Even rolls, if made large and not too thick, may be toasted after being sliced through gently. The covering crust holds each half together.

- 1 cup rice bran
  ½ cup brown-rice flour
  ½ cup arrowroot flour
  ¾ teaspoon bicarbonate of soda
  1½ teaspoons cream of tartar
  1¼ cups chicken stock

- 1 cup rice bran
  1 cup brown-rice flour
  ¾ teaspoon bicarbonate of soda
  1½ teaspoons cream of tartar
  1¼ cups chicken stock
  1 tablespoon lemon juice (optional)
  1 heaped tablespoon margarine, melted

The method for both recipes is simply to sift and mix the dry ingredients, then add liquids and beat till smooth with a wooden spoon. Spoon the dough (it has a very soft consistency, so it will spread and not be too thick) in heaped tablespoonfuls, or desired size, close together in baking pan or tray. Bake at 190°C (375°F) for about one hour or until lightly browned. These rolls do not freeze well, so make small quantities. Makes 8-10 rolls.

Rolls

Use any of the above bread mixtures to make rolls, but add slightly more liquid to make a softer, dropping batter rather than a stiff dough. Even the rye-oat mixture does not need the waterbath method of baking if baked as rolls. Bake rolls at 190°C (375°F) for about one hour or until browned. Before baking, rolls may be brushed with water or milk and a sprinkling of sesame seeds added over the tops if liked. Rolls freeze well.

Savoury Muffins

1½ cups flour (any combination tolerated)
¼ teaspoon pepper
¾ teaspoon bicarbonate of soda
1½ teaspoons cream of tartar
1 egg or extra ¼ cup goat's or soya milk
¾ cup goat's or soya milk
3 tablespoons melted margarine
1 small grated onion
2 teaspoons lemon juice
½ cup sesame seeds (optional)
extra sesame seeds for tops

Sift the flour with the pepper, soda and cream of tartar. Mix in beaten egg, milk, margarine, onion, lemon juice and ½ cup sesame seeds (if used); mix well. Bake as for rolls, or in patty tins if small muffins are needed, at 200°C (400°F) for 30-40 minutes—reduce the baking time for small muffins. Makes 9-12 muffins.

Try these as a change from sweet rolls. They are delicious with salads or soups, in packed lunches, or at morning tea. They freeze well, but do separate them first if you want to use them only a few at a time.

Two variations on the basic recipe are:

• Onion and Bacon Muffins: to the above mixture add ¾ cup finely chopped bacon, if tolerated. Use only fresh, sugar-free bacon.
• Herbed Muffins: to the above mixture add —
  ½ cup chopped parsley
  1 cup young beansprouts
  3 teaspoons finely chopped chives
  2 extra tablespoons grated onion

Crispbreads

Crispbreads may be used in school lunches or as a base for snacks. See "Crispbreads" in Chapter 2, p. 28, and also waffle crispbread made with any grain you can tolerate, Chapter 9, p. 94.

Fruit Buns or Raisin Bread

Since first sampling homemade raisin bread, the insipid commercial sort has never been over our doorstep. Homemade raisin bread is much more satisfying and you are in control of how much spice and fruit you add.

To any of the above recipes for bread or rolls, or any you have devised yourself, simply add, for each kilogram of flour, 2 cups (or less) sultanas and/or currants, and sifted with the flours, 3½ teaspoons of mixed spice and 2 teaspoons cinnamon (less if preferred, though non-wheat flour can take a lot of spice). The liquid for fruit bread could well be fruit juice or juice and water rather than milk. The loaves or buns may be glazed if liked (see Chapter 14, p. 200).

Hot-cross Buns

See recipes in Chapter 14, p. 197.

8
SANDWICH
SPREADS

With the common allergy to yeast, the usual and very convenient options of processed luncheon meats and vegemite are out and most likely cheese also. Others may be allergic to eggs. If the allergy is to cow's milk, there are goat's and sheep's cheeses available, but these may prove rather expensive for everyday use if the family is large. What, then, can one use in sandwiches for casual meals or in school lunches, particularly when they must (according to my children) look like the other children's sandwiches? The following are a few suggestions. All are yeast-free.

Curd Cheeses

Goat's-milk Cottage Cheese

> 2 plain junket tablets
> 1 tablespoon cold water
> 5 cups milk

Crush the junket tablets and dissolve them in the water. Warm the milk to blood heat and remove from heat; add junket solution and stir thoroughly but briefly. Cover the saucepan and let the mixture stand in a warm place until set. Cut through the junket with a knife, then strain off whey through muslin. Allow curds to drain by suspending the muslin bag for several hours or overnight. The longer the draining time, the drier and less creamy the cottage cheese and the smaller the volume. I simply suspend the bag inside a deep saucepan with a small diameter with the lid jammed on tightly over the ends of the muslin, which are wound around the handle, and then place the saucepan in the refrigerator so the cheese is chilled while draining (see Figure 2). Pour off excess whey from the saucepan as it collects in the bottom. Five cups (1 litre) milk makes approximately 1²/₃ cups (400 g) creamy cottage cheese *or* 1 cup (300 g) of firmer cheese, depending on the time it is allowed to drain.

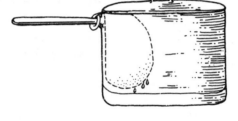

Figure 2 Goat's-milk cottage cheese: saucepan-drip method.

Soya-bean Cheese (Tofu)

3 cups soya beans
13 cups water
2 dessertspoons Epsom salts or ngari

Soak the soya beans overnight, then rinse thoroughly. Crush beans or blend with 2 cups of water; add 11 cups of water and bring to the boil. Simmer for up to 30 minutes, then strain through a muslin bag or stocking. Retain the fluid and heat to boiling point, then remove from stove and add the Epsom salts or ngari (dissolved in hot water); stir in gently. Leave till thoroughly curded (approximately 15 minutes), then strain through a muslin bag and refrigerate. Makes about three cups.

Here are some ways in which curd cheese may be used:

• Plain—a bland creamy spread. Add slices of cooked fresh beetroot, tomato, cucumber, capsicum, etcetera, or banana slices dipped in lemon juice, if using plain in sandwiches. A children's favourite is to sprinkle some sultanas, if allowed, over the cheese.

• Make spreads—add walnuts and celery, both chopped, and mix well; or add banana mashed with a squeeze of lemon juice; or add chopped dried fruit, such as prunes, raisins, sultanas or dates.

Nut Butters

Soya-bean Butter

250 g (8 oz) raw soya beans
2 tablespoons oil (any except peanut oil if being used as a peanut substitute)

Soak soya beans overnight and drain. Place them in large saucepan and cover with water, simmer until softened and drain. Spread on large oven trays and roast in a moderate oven until just browned evenly—take care not to scorch them. When just browned, they taste like peanuts; when overcooked, they taste bitter. Place 1-2 cupfuls of roasted beans in an electric blender, and grind on high speed in short bursts. Then add oil gradually until desired consistency is reached. Store in the refrigerator. Makes about three cups.

Soya-bean butter can be used: straight as a peanut butter substitute; or combined with mashed banana as a spread; or in recipes calling for peanut butter.

Peanut Butter

> 500 g (1 lb) raw peanuts or roasted unsalted if fresh
> 4 tablespoons oil (peanut or soya oil would keep the food family
>   consistent)
> dash of lemon juice to season

Roast peanuts, if necessary, in a moderate oven, then grind to a
flour in an electric blender. While blender is on, add oil
gradually until desired consistency is reached. Season to taste
and store in the refrigerator. Makes about two cups.

There are commercial nut and seed butters available now,
free from sugar, salt, artificial additives and added oils. Check
for these at your health-food store. Some varieties, such as
almond paste, are expensive but delicious and useful to have.
Store them in the refrigerator.

Savoury Spreads

The next two recipes show variations on the one basic idea: the
first has breadcrumbs and cottage cheese to thicken it; the other
has egg.

Tomato Spread

> 1 large tomato
> ½ cup soft breadcrumbs (from tolerated bread)
> 1 grated onion
> 2 tablespoons goat's cottage cheese (recipe p. 87) or tofu (recipe p. 88)
> ½ teaspoon mixed herbs
> ¼ cup water

Place tomato, crumbs, onion, cottage cheese and herbs into a
saucepan, then add the water; cook gently until mixture
softens. Leave till cold before using. Makes ¾ cup.

Mock Chicken (cheese-free)

For recipe see Chapter 2, p. 28.

Savoury Chicken (cheese-free)

small quantity of white sauce (about 1 cup)
1 finely chopped onion
1 finely chopped green pepper
oil
cooked diced chicken
finely chopped parsley

Make the white sauce using allowable milk or soya milk or chicken stock and allowable thickener (see Chapter 3). Sauté onion and pepper in the oil until softened and lightly tinted. Add onion, pepper and chicken to white sauce and add parsley. Mix well and chill before using. Prepare as soon as possible after the chicken is cooked, and freeze in suitably sized portions if it is not all to be used straight away.

Jams

Almost any fruit—fresh, frozen or unsweetened tinned—may be made into a jam or spread. Simply gently stew the fruit with a little liquid. Add gelatine for a jellied jam or thicken with a little arrowroot for a fruit spread. Sweeten only if necessary. Purée if a smooth jam is desired. Store in the refrigerator or freeze in small amounts—the pectin in jam inhibits mould. Most commercial pectin also contains sugar; however, adding a liberal amount of sliced apple to the other fruit when stewing the jam has the same effect and the apple can be removed when cooking is completed.

Cherry Jam

See Chapter 3, p. 47.

Honey Caramel Spread

For those who can tolerate honey: see Chapter 3, p. 46.

Apricot Jam

> 250 g (8 oz) fresh or frozen apricots or 125 g (4 oz) unsulphured
> dried apricots
> ¾ cup water
> 1 teaspoon gelatine
> fructose or honey or Equal (optional)

Gently stew the apricots in the water. Add the gelatine mixed with a little hot water, and stir until gelatine is dissolved. Remove from heat, sweeten with fructose, honey or Equal in small amounts if necessary, or purée some sultanas in with the jam. Bottle the jam—it will thicken on cooling—and spread, when cold, on sandwiches, toast, scones or pikelets, or use in cakes, slices and puddings. Makes about two cups.

Apple Jam

> 3 eating apples, such as Delicious
> unsweetened apple juice, freshly juiced or tinned
> ½ teaspoon (or to taste) cinnamon or a pinch ground cloves or
> ginger

Peel and slice apples and place them in saucepan with 1 cup of juice. Cover and simmer until the apples are soft; add spices to taste. Purée jam and add gelatine as in Apricot Jam, if necessary, to thicken it. Makes about two cups.

9
BATTERS, PASTRIES AND PASTA

This is a basic section, in the true sense, for those with grain allergies, as batters, pastries and pasta form the necessary base to many dishes, both savoury and sweet. They are also a change from breads, potato and simple boiled rice.

If you can still have your favourite tart filling or are craving spaghetti and meatballs Italian style, but you are allergic to wheat, then the following ideas will help you. The recipes aim to be palatable to all so you will not have to make separate meals for different members of the family or guests. Egg-free recipes are given for waffles, pancakes, pikelets and pastry.

Waffle Batter

Waffles are universally popular. They are useful to those with grain and/or dairy allergies, as waffle batter may be made with almost any flour, and soya milk, fruit juice or mineral water can be used instead of cow's or goat's milk. You do, of course, need a waffle iron. Note that arrowroot, cornflour or potato flour are included in all the recipes.

Plain Waffle Crispbread

To make a crispbread use any of the following recipes but preferably use goat's or soya milk, water or soda water rather than the sweeter juices. When cooled, either freeze for later use or store for a short time in airtight containers. Before using as a crispbread, recrisp waffles in a moderately hot oven or in the toaster. Once recrisped, waffles will stay crisp. Such crispbread can be useful for school lunches as well as a base for snacks.

For non-wheat waffles, an increase in the number of eggs and/or in the amount of liquid may be necessary. Egg-free waffles are possible too: see recipe on p. 97.

The following recipes contain no sweeteners since there is usually sufficient sweetness in the toppings added to dessert waffles. You may add some if you wish; about 1 teaspoon of fructose, a little more honey or 1 tablespoon of sultanas liquefied with the liquid ingredient.

Wheat-flour Waffle Batter

> *2 eggs*
> *125 g (4 oz) melted margarine*
> *1 teaspoon vanilla essence*
> *¾ cup goat's or soya milk or unsweetened fruit juice*
> *½ cup water*
> *2 cups wholewheat flour*
> *1 tablespoon arrowroot or 2 tablespoons cornflour or potato flour*
> *1 teaspoon bicarbonate of soda*
> *2 teaspoons cream of tartar*

Mix the eggs and liquid ingredients, beating well. Gradually add the flour sifted with the other dry ingredients, and mix well. Cook on a hot greased waffle iron. Makes 8-10 waffles.

Wholly Rice-grain Waffle Batter

3 eggs
125 g (4 oz) melted margarine
1 teaspoon vanilla essence
1¼ cups goat's or soya milk
1 cup of water or unsweetened fruit juice
1 cup brown-rice flour
1 cup rice bran
1 tablespoon arrowroot
1 teaspoon bicarbonate of soda
2 teaspoons cream of tartar

Mix the eggs and the liquid ingredients, beating well.
Gradually add the flour sifted with the other dry ingredients,
mixing well. Cook on a hot greased waffle iron. Makes 8-10
waffles.

Soya-rice Waffle Batter

3 eggs
125 g (4 oz) melted margarine
1 teaspoon vanilla essence
½-1 cup water or unsweetened fruit juice
1¼ cups goat's or soya milk
½ cup rice bran ⎫
½ cup brown-rice flour ⎬ (for the required 2 cups of flour)
1 cup soya flour ⎭
1 tablespoon arrowroot
1 teaspoon bicarbonate of soda
2 teaspoons cream of tartar

Mix the eggs and the liquid ingredients, beating well.
Gradually add the flour sifted with the other dry ingredients,
mixing well. Cook on a hot greased waffle iron.

If the soya flour taste is too strong for you, increase the
amount of vanilla essence. Makes 8-10 waffles.

Soya-oat Waffle Batter

> 2 eggs, separated
> 1¼ cups goat's or soya milk
> 1 cup water or unsweetened fruit juice
> 1 teaspoon vanilla essence
> 1¼ cups soya flour
> ¾ cup fine oatmeal
> 2 teaspoons cream of tartar
> 1 tablespoon arrowroot
> 1 teaspoon bicarbonate of soda
> 125 g (4 oz) melted margarine

An alternative method of mixing waffles is to separate the eggs. Beat the egg yolks until light, then add the milk, water or juice and vanilla; beat until smooth. Sift the dry ingredients and add the egg and milk mixture and the melted margarine, beating well. Fold in stiffly beaten eggwhites, and allow to stand for 10 minutes before cooking on a greased hot waffle iron. Makes 8-10 waffles.

Arrowroot Waffle Batter

> 1 cup arrowroot
> ½ teaspoon vanilla essence
> ⅔ cup mineral or soda water
> 3 eggs, separated

Mix all ingredients, except eggwhites, until the batter is smooth. Fold in stiffly beaten eggwhites and bake on hot greased waffle iron. Makes about 5 waffles.

Egg-free Waffle Batter

⅓ cup potato flour or arrowroot
⅔ cup rye, soya or other flour or rice bran
½ teaspoon bicarbonate of soda
1 teaspoon cream of tartar
1¼ cups goat's or soya milk
2½ tablespoons melted margarine

Sift the dry ingredients and add the milk, mixing well. Gradually stir in the melted margarine. Cook on a hot greased waffle iron (make sure the iron is really hot before adding the mixture). Makes 5-6 waffles.

Ideally, waffles should be served while still hot, and may be topped with any of the following:

- Thick stewed fruit, such as apples, apricots, blackberries.
- Honey Caramel Sauce, p. 46.
- Jam Spread, p. 91, with or without a scraping of margarine first.
- Cherry Sauce, p. 47.
- Goat's Cheese Mock Cream, p. 154, added to any of the above.
- Goat's Milk Ice-cream, p. 174, or other allowable ice-cream.
- Thick Banana Topping or other fruit topping, pp. 172-174.

Pancakes

If you make pancakes often, and eggs are not amongst your allergy foods, then an automatic pancake-maker would be a good investment—it produces fine pancakes and can cope with non-wheat flours. All the following recipes, except where stated otherwise, have been made successfully on an automatic pancake-maker. Alternatively, use a small frying pan or the special crêpe pans.

Unfilled pancakes (or crêpes) may be frozen: place a sheet of waxed or greaseproof paper between each pancake in the stack, place the stack in a plastic bag, then remove air, seal and freeze them on a flat surface. They must, of course, be thawed completely if they are to be rolled up, but not if being used as lasagne or in a pancake-layered gateau. Treat frozen pancakes gently as they are thin and break easily.

As well as being a good substitute for lasagne pasta, pancakes can take the place of cannelloni; and when rolled without a filling and sliced across fairly thinly, they can be used as noodles too. Also, a homemade sausage with a pancake wrapped around it, then sliced into suitable-sized segments and the pancake held firm with a toothpick, makes an excellent sausage roll for a birthday party or adult party.

In all these recipes extra margarine for cooking is needed. If pancakes are to be used for a dessert, 1 teaspoon of vanilla essence and ½ teaspoon grated lemon rind may be added to the basic batter, and an appropriate unsweetened fruit juice used instead of milk. If pancakes are to be used with a savoury filling, 1½ tablespoons of toasted or raw sesame seeds may be added to the batter.

Consistency of the batter is important—it should be about the consistency of thick heavy cream. Adjust the liquid to suit: if a slightly firmer pancake is needed for more substantial fillings, such as diced meats, then reduce the liquid a little to make a thicker batter. Add more liquid to the batter if it thickens too much during cooking.

Wholewheat Pancakes

1 cup fine wholewheat flour
1 tablespoon melted margarine
3 60 g eggs
1¼-1½ cups goat's or soya milk

Place the flour in a bowl, make a well in the centre and add the melted margarine, eggs and half the milk, and beat well with a wooden spoon until smooth. Mix in the remaining milk. Cover the batter and leave to stand for 30 minutes (this makes more tender pancakes). Makes 12-16 pancakes.

Cornmeal Pancakes

½ cup fine yellow cornmeal
½ cup boiling water
3 eggs
½ cup soya flour or fine oatmeal
2 tablespoons melted margarine
½-¾ cup goat's or soya milk

Combine the cornmeal and water and stir until smooth. Allow to cool slightly, then add the eggs, flour and margarine. Mix till smooth, then add the milk gradually until the desired consistency is reached. Makes 12-16 pancakes.

Buckwheat Pancakes

⅔ cup buckwheat flour
3 tablespoons melted margarine
1 egg
1 cup or more goat's or soya milk
1 teaspoon vanilla essence (if a dessert pancake)

Place the flour in a bowl, make a well in the centre and add the melted margarine, egg and half the milk, and beat well until smooth. Mix in the remaining milk. Cover the batter and leave to stand for 30 minutes. Makes 12-16 pancakes.

Soya-rice Pancakes

¾ cup soya flour
¼ cup brown-rice flour or rice bran
1 tablespoon melted margarine
2 eggs
1½ cups goat's or soya milk

Place the flour in a bowl, make a well in the centre and add the melted margarine, eggs and half the milk; beat well until smooth. Mix in the remaining milk. Cover the batter and leave to stand for 30 minutes. Makes 12-16 pancakes.

Whole-rye Pancakes

½ cup rye flour
1 tablespoon melted margarine
1 egg
1 cup goat's milk or 1 cup of water and 2 tablespoons soya milk

Place the flour in a bowl, make a well in the centre and add the melted margarine, egg and half the milk; beat well until smooth. Mix in the remaining milk. Cover the batter and leave to stand for 30 minutes. Makes 12-16 pancakes.

Wholly Rice Pancakes

½ cup rice bran
½ cup brown-rice flour
2 tablespoons melted margarine
2 eggs
1¼-1½ cups goat's or soya milk

Place the bran and flour in a bowl, make a well in the centre and add the melted margarine, eggs and half the milk; beat well until smooth. Mix in the remaining milk, cover the batter and leave to stand for 30 minutes.

This recipe makes a thin lacey pancake on an automatic pancake-maker. Keep the batter well stirred between dippings as settling may occur. Alternatively, use a crêpe pan or frying pan for a thicker pancake—the thicker pancakes tend to break more easily when rolled than the thin rice ones, but are good for pancake gateaus. Replacing ¼ cup of brown-rice flour with ¼ cup arrowroot will make a less delicate pancake. Makes 12-16 pancakes.

Egg-free Pancakes

Use the Egg-free Waffle Batter recipe on p. 97, but increase the amount of liquid to give a thinner pancake-batter consistency. Cook in a pan, not an automatic pancake-maker. Pour in a tablespoon or more of the batter and tip pan quickly to spread the batter into a thin round. This batter may even be tossed!

Also see Oat-flour Pikelets, p. 103, but make the batter thinner for pancakes by adding extra oil, milk or water. Cook, as above, in a pan. See also Coconut Pikelets, p. 102.

Pancake Fillings

Use any of your favourite recipes, adapted if necessary, to fill the pancakes. Savoury fillings include diced meats and poultry; hardboiled eggs; spinach or silver beet; allowable cottage cheese or white sauce, with onions, herbs and selected spices, according to your preference.

For dessert pancake fillings see Chapter 13, pp. 166-169.

Pikelets or Drop Scones

Again, all these recipes are sweetener-free since the topping they are served with usually provides adequate sweetness. If a sweeter batter is required add either 1-2 teaspoons fructose, *or* 1 tablespoon sultanas liquefied in a blender with some of the liquid ingredients.

Soya-flour Pikelets

²/₃ cup soya flour
1 dessertspoon brown-rice flour
½ teaspoon bicarbonate of soda
1 teaspoon cream of tartar
2 eggs, separated
1 tablespoon melted margarine
1 cup goat's or soya milk or water
1 teaspoon vanilla essence

Sift into a mixing bowl the flours, soda and cream of tartar; make a well in the centre of the flour and add the egg yolks, melted margarine, milk and vanilla. Beat until smooth, then fold in the stiffly beaten eggwhites.

Pikelet cooking method: Heat a large pan or fry-pan, grease with a little margarine, and drop dessertspoonfuls of the mixture into the pan and cook until bubbles appear. Turn over with a spatula and brown on the other side. Cool the pikelets, wrapped in a clean teatowel. Makes about 30 pikelets.

Cottage Cheese Pikelets

> 3 eggs, separated
> 125 g (4 oz) soft, fresh soya or goat's cottage cheese
> ¼ cup flour, such as brown-rice flour, oatmeal, rye, millet, soya
>   flour
> ¼ teaspoon cinnamon
> 1 tablespoon oil (optional)

Blend the egg yolks with the cheese, flour and cinnamon. Whisk the eggwhites until stiff but not dry and fold them gently into the cheese mixture; add oil (if used) and mix through. Cook in the usual way (see above). Makes about 20 pikelets.

Coconut Pikelets

> 2 cups water
> 1½ tablespoons oil
> 1 cup soya or brown-rice flour (or other tolerated flour)
> 1 cup desiccated coconut
> ¾ teaspoon bicarbonate of soda ⎱ or 3 teaspoons corn-free
> 1½ teaspoons cream of tartar ⎰   baking powder

Blend all ingredients in an electric blender until just mixed. Cook in the usual way (see above) in dessertspoonfuls, or large quantities if a pancake is required. Makes about 30 pikelets.

Oat-flour Pikelets

1 cup fine oatmeal
½ teaspoon bicarbonate of soda ⎫ or 2 teaspoons corn-free
1 teaspoon cream of tartar ⎭ baking powder
1 tablespoon oil
¾ cup goat's or soya milk
1 60 g egg or 2 tablespoons water or extra 1 tablespoon oil

Sift the flour, soda and cream of tartar, make a well in the flour and add the remaining ingredients; beat until smooth. Cook in the usual way (see p. 102). Makes about 30 pikelets.

Buckwheat Pikelets

1 cup buckwheat flour
½ teaspoon bicarbonate of soda
1 teaspoon cream of tartar
1⅓ cups mineral or soda water
1 teaspoon vanilla essence
2 tablespoons oil

Sift the flour with soda and cream of tartar, add all remaining ingredients and beat well until bubbly. Cook in the usual way (see p. 102). Makes about 30 pikelets.

Potato Pikelets

2 cups potato flour
½ teaspoon bicarbonate of soda
1 teaspoon cream of tartar
1 egg
½ teaspoon honey or fructose (optional)
water

Sift the dry ingredients, add the egg and sweetener (if used) and mix quickly to a smooth paste, adding enough water to make a very thick batter. Cook in the usual way (see p. 102). Makes about 30 pikelets.

Rice-flour Pikelets

⅓ cup brown-rice flour
⅓ cup arrowroot
⅓ cup rice bran
½ teaspoon bicarbonate of soda
1 teaspoon cream of tartar
2 eggs, separated
1 tablespoon melted margarine
¾-1 cup goat's or soya milk, or water
1 teaspoon vanilla essence

Make as for Soya-flour Pikelets (see p. 102). The mixture may appear runny but this is correct for the rice-flour version. Makes about 40 pikelets.

Preferably, pikelets should be served fresh and warm, spread with margarine and topped with any of the following. Pikelets may also be frozen.

- Thick, stewed and puréed fresh fruit, such as apples, apricots.
- Fruit jams and spreads, p. 91.
- Honey Caramel Sauce, p. 46.
- Goat's Cheese Mock Cream, p. 154, or other topping, see Chapter 12.

Pastry

The quantities given in the following recipes are for a large flan tin (approximately 25 centimetres or 10 inches in diameter). The flours specified are given as a guide only, but the proportions of flour, margarine and liquid are important to produce the particular type of pastry in each case.

I find a plastic pastry mat invaluable when rolling out non-wheat pastries and inverting them over the tin or pie plate. The mat can then be peeled off the pastry rather than vice versa, which is not always easy to do. If you do not have one of the special pastry mats or sheets, use a sheet of greaseproof paper or waxed lunch wrap. I suggest that the tart tin or plate be inverted over the rolled-out pastry first and then the whole thing turned right side up and the sheet peeled off the pastry—any cracks in the pastry can then be repaired. Some unbeaten eggwhite rolled around the inside of the pastry case to coat it just before baking can help to seal it. If you find the pastry rather sticky to roll out despite adding enough flour, try rolling it between two sheets of greaseproof paper.

Uncooked tart cases can be filled and placed for the first 15 minutes baking time in a hot to very hot oven to seal the pastry; the oven temperature is then reduced for the remainder of the cooking time. Alternatively, bake the case blind, either completely or partially. Place a piece of greaseproof paper on the bottom of the case, weighted down with a few dry lentils or rice to maintain the shape of the case. Bake at 190°C (375°F) until cooked to the desired degree. Cooked tart cases may be frozen, but they are fragile.

To help with conversions in pastry recipes, I have included a table of weights and cup measures for each of the most commonly used non-wheat flours. See "Cooking Notes", pp. 11-12.

Flaky Pie Pastry

185 g margarine
1½ cups flour
¼ cup or more iced water

For the flour, the following are suggested:

1 cup rye flour
½ cup arrowroot } or

¾ cup soya flour
½ cup oatmeal } or
¼ cup rolled oats

1 cup soya flour
½ cup arrowroot }

Cut the margarine into the flour with a knife. Add the iced water gradually and mix with your fingers into a ball of dough —add more water if necessary to make a pliable dough. Allow dough to rest for half an hour before rolling out. Brush pastry top with water, milk or beaten egg before baking. The pastry may be used for double crusts and may be used in steak and kidney pies, mince pies, sausage rolls and savoury tarts.

Do not roll the pastry too thinly if it is to be rolled up, for example, with sausage rolls, or if it needs to form a sound case, as in party mince pies. When making sausage rolls from home-made sausages, frozen sausages (not pork) may be used if they are skinless. The pastry wrapped around the suitably sized frozen sausages then has a chance to cook and seal before the juices from the meat can ooze out. This recipe makes about 500 g (1 lb) of pastry.

Savoury Tart Pastry

125 g (4 oz) margarine
1½ cups flour
¼ cup or more cold water

Cut the margarine into the flour with a knife. Add the cold water gradually and mix with your fingers into a dough—add more water if necessary.

These are the basic proportions; note the different liquid amounts used. The dough should be soft and readily pliable. This pastry is suitable for single crusts (bottom layer) only.

Soya-rice Tart Pastry

⅔ cup soya flour
1 cup rice bran or ½ cup rice bran and ⅓ cup brown-rice flour
125 g (4 oz) margarine
½ teaspoon kelp powder (optional)
¼-½ cup cold water

Either rub the margarine into the flour and kelp with your finger tips and add sufficient water to form a firm but pliable dough ball, kneading well; *or* place flour, kelp and margarine in a food processor bowl and process for a few seconds until mixed

—add cold water gradually down the feed tube until a pliable ball is formed. Only a little, if any, extra kneading by hand is necessary when using a food processor. Roll out pastry to fit the tin or plate.

Whole-rye Tart Pastry

1⅓ cups rye flour
125 g (4 oz) margarine
3-4 tablespoons cold water

Either of the methods outlined above under Soya-rice Tart Pastry may be used.

Rye-oat Tart Pastry

1 cup rye flour
1 cup ground oats or oatmeal
125 g (4 oz) margarine
4-5 tablespoons cold water

Either of the methods outlined above under Soya-rice Tart Pastry may be used.

Rye-rice Tart Pastry

⅔ cup rye flour
½ cup rice bran
½ cup arrowroot
125 g (4 oz) margarine
2 tablespoons cold water

Either of the methods outlined above under Soya-rice Tart Pastry may be used.

Dessert Tart Pastry

²/₃ cup soya flour
1 cup rice bran
60 g (2 oz) margarine
1 egg
1 teaspoon fructose (optional)
¼-½ cup cold water (or unsweetened fruit juice and omit the fructose)

Either place all the ingredients except the water in a food processor and process until mixed; then add sufficient water while motor is running for a pliable ball to form. Alternatively, rub the margarine into the flour until mixture resembles breadcrumbs; add egg and fructose and sufficient water to form a pliable dough ball; knead well. Allow to rest for 30 minutes before rolling out.

This is a basic recipe which produces a hard pastry. For more of a crumb-case pastry, use brown-rice flour in place of, or in a proportion with, the rice bran. The recipe makes sufficient for a 25 cm (10 in) tart.

Two variations for fruit and other dessert tarts:

* For a 23 cm (9 in) tin:.
    180 g (6 oz) flour, for example, ²/₃ cup soya flour and ⅓ cup brown-rice flour
    ¼ teaspoon bicarbonate of soda
    ½ teaspoon cream of tartar
    110 g (3½ oz) margarine
    1 teaspoon fructose or 1 dessertspoon sultanas liquefied with the water
    30 g (1 oz) shredded almonds
    ½ teaspoon grated lemon rind
    1 egg yolk
    2 teaspoons lemon juice
    1 tablespoon cold water

Sift the flour, soda and cream of tartar and rub into margarine until the mixture is crumbly. Add the fructose, almonds and lemon rind. Mix together the egg yolk, lemon juice and water and lightly mix them into the flour with a knife. Add more water if necessary for the dough to hold together. Knead lightly into a round. Cover and allow to stand for 30 minutes before rolling out.

- For an 18 cm (7 in) flan:
    - ½ cup soya or rye flour
    - ⅛ cup potato flour or arrowroot
    - ½ teaspoon mixed spice
    - 45 g (1½ oz) margarine
    - ⅛ cup rolled oats
    - 1 teaspoon fructose or 1 dessertspoon sultanas liquefied with the milk
    - 3-4 tablespoons goat's or soya milk

Sift flours and the spice, rub in the margarine, stir in the oats and fructose and bind with the milk. Roll out the pastry to fit the base of an 18 cm (7 in) flan tin and place dough in the tin. Ease the pastry up the sides of the tin with your fingertips.

Slice Pastry

For a soft but firm "cakey" pastry base, see Crostata Slice, p. 151. For a thinner slice base, see Apricot Almond Slice, p. 143.

Pasta

Additive-free commercial varieties of pasta—spaghetti, noodles and lasagne—thankfully now exist. There are commercially available wholewheat spaghetti, macaroni and lasagne, soya-flour macaroni, triticale spaghetti and noodles, and mixed seven-grain spaghetti and lasagne. Read the labels carefully if you are on a salt-free diet.

It is certainly possible to make pasta at home if you wish. I recommend *Pasta Cookbook* (Sunset Books, Lane Publishing Co., 1980) as an inexpensive but comprehensive book. It gives recipes using non-wheat flours. A hand pasta machine is recommended for those who intend to make a lot of pasta themselves. It also is easier to roll out more thinly some of the non-wheat flours using a machine rather than a rolling pin.

Here is a rye-flour pasta recipe for those unable to eat the commercially available range of pastas. It is difficult to make pasta with rice flour—commercial rice vermicelli may be used as a substitute, but remember that it is a white-rice product.

Rye Pasta

2 cups rye flour
2 60 g eggs
1½ tablespoons oil
about 3-5 tablespoons water

If you're using a food processor, process the flour and eggs briefly with a metal blade until the mixture is crumbly. Then add the oil and water gradually down the feed tube, with the motor running, until a pliable dough forms. Add an extra tablespoon of flour if the dough is sticky, or small amounts (teaspoons) of water if the dough is dry. Turn dough out onto a floured surface and knead for two-three minutes. If the dough is to be rolled with a rolling pin, cover and leave it to rest for 30 minutes. If you are using a pasta machine, you may proceed immediately.

If you're making the dough by hand, sift the flour onto a board or workbench, make a well in the centre and add the eggs. Whisk the eggs lightly with a fork, adding a little water and gradually draw in the flour around the edges. Add water when necessary and mix until a soft but not sticky dough is formed. Knead the dough well on a clean floured work surface, until it is soft and elastic (anything up to 10 minutes or so). Let the dough rest for 30 minutes before rolling out. Divide the dough in four portions, rolling each separately—roll out to a rectangle about 3 mm (⅛ in) thick. Leave each rolled portion to dry out a little on a floured teatowel or pastry sheet. To make noodles, roll up each piece and cut them into the required width strips with a sharp knife. Alternatively, simply slice the flat sheet into thin strips with a sharp knife—more time-consuming but the dough is easier to handle.

Cook in plenty of boiling water until just softened and serve immediately. Makes 3½ cups cooked medium-width noodles.

10
BISCUITS AND
COOKIES

The emphasis in this chapter, as in the rest of the book, is on non-wheat biscuits. Most of the recipes began as wheat-flour recipes, so use it if you are able and prefer it. If you do, omit any extra eggwhite given in a recipe as it is used as an extra binding agent when using non-wheat flours. Non-wheat flours often require longer cooking time, so again adjust this if you are using wheat flour. Carob is used in the following recipes, but if you prefer and can tolerate it, cocoa may be used (see "Ingredients": "Carob" and also "Cocoa", p. 14).

Steps in the adapting process are shown for some recipes to give you a few ideas. Do try your own flour combinations too.

Some useful generalities when adapting biscuit recipes are:

• If using rice flour, use rice bran as well for a less crumbly result.
• When using soya flour, use only full-fat soya flour in these recipes.
• Extra eggwhite, beaten stiffly and then folded in last or simply added with the other eggs, will help bind crumbly biscuits, as will the gelatine mixture for those who are allergic to eggs. (See "Egg Substitutes in Baking", p. 15.)

• In any "rolled oat" recipe, try an allowable rolled grain in place of the oats, such as wheat, barley, rye, rice (also known as rice flakes) and soya flakes, or the commercially available wholegrain puffed wheat or puffed brown-rice cereals, free from added salt and sugar. To soften rice flakes, place in boiling water so that they are just covered and leave for a moment before draining and using in the recipe.

• Many biscuits with fruit juice or fruit in them (fresh or dried) may not need added sweetener. If some is needed, select from:
—fructose—1-2 dessertspoons per batch of biscuits;
—honey—1-2 tablespoons or to taste per batch of biscuits, either creamed in with the margarine if only a little honey (1 tablespoon or so), or blended with and added together with any melted ingredient, such as the margarine or copha;
—sultanas—¼-½ cup per 2 cups of flour; liquefly them in a blender with a liquid ingredient, such as the milk, juice or yoghurt, tofu or cottage cheese, or stewed fruit; they may not be suited to all biscuit recipes.

• If substituting carob for cocoa, increase the quantity of carob for a stronger flavour. Carob imparts a natural sweetness, unlike cocoa, so adjust other sweeteners accordingly.

• Try using your allowable toasted muesli (see recipes in Chapter 6, p. 65) without dried fruit in recipes calling for cornflakes, or use straight rice flakes or millet flakes.

• When using non-wheat flours, particularly those with a more definite flavour, such as rye, soya, buckwheat or millet, be prepared to substantially increase the amount of spice or other flavourings. See the substitutions in the Bran Macaroon recipe, p. 120, for an example of this.

• Cornflour, arrowroot and potato flour are more useful in biscuits for a crunchy, finer product than some of the other non-wheat flours.

• For wheat bran, substitute rolled non-wheat grains. Rice bran is not equivalent since it gives a much smoother texture than wheat bran.

• See "Egg Substitutes in Baking", p. 15, for substitutes that can be used in the biscuit recipes in this chapter.

Banana Oat Biscuits

¾ cup margarine
1 cup sugar
1 egg
1¾ cups oats
1 cup mashed banana
½ cup chopped nuts
1½ cups plain flour
½ teaspoon bicarbonate of soda
¾ teaspoon cinnamon
½ teaspoon salt

Cream the margarine and sugar and add the egg; beat thoroughly. Fold in the oats, bananas and nuts. Stir in the sifted dry ingredients. Spoon teaspoonfuls of the mixture onto a greased oven tray, leaving a little space between each. Bake for 15 minutes in a hot oven, 200°C (400°F), until browned; then cool on a wire rack. Makes about 36 biscuits.

This recipe was then adapted in the following ways (all recipes may be made egg-free by replacing the egg with the gelatine mixture):

Sugar-free

¾ cup margarine
1 dessertspoon fructose
   or 1 tablespoon honey
   (optional)
1 egg
1¾ cups oats
1 cup mashed banana
½ cup chopped nuts
1½ cups wholewheat flour
¾ teaspoon cinnamon or
   mixed spice
½ teaspoon bicarbonate of soda
omit salt

Wheat-free

As for the sugar-free adaptation, except for:

{ ¾ cup rye flour
{ ¾ cup rice bran or arrowroot

Oat-free 1

Both as for the sugar-free recipe above, except for:

> ½ cup margarine
> 1 egg plus 1 white
>   (added with egg)
> 1¾ cups rolled rice

> ¾ cup rye flour ⎫
> ¾ cup rice bran ⎬

Oat-free 2

> ½ cup margarine
> 1 egg plus 1 white
>   (added with egg)
> 1½ cups rolled rice (an
>   extra ¼ cup rice bran
>   included to make same
>   total amount of flour)

> ⎧ 1 cup rice bran
> ⎨ ½ cup soya flour
> ⎩ ¼ cup brown-rice flour

Wholly Rice 1

As for the Oat-free 1 recipe, except for:
1 cup rice bran
½ cup brown-rice flour

Wholly Rice 2

As for the Oat-free 1 recipe, except for:
¾ cup rolled rice
2½ cups puffed brown rice
1 teaspoon cinnamon
¼ teaspoon mixed spice

Carob Crackles

> 3 cups rolled rice or puffed wheat or puffed brown rice or
>   crumbled brown rice wafers
> 2 cups coconut
> 5 tablespoons carob or 3 tablespoons cocoa
> 1 dessertspoon fructose or 1 tablespoon honey
> 250 g (8 oz) copha

Mix the dry ingredients thoroughly in a mixing bowl; add the melted copha (mixed with honey if used). Stir well to coat dry ingredients, then spoon into paper cases and chill until set. Makes about 24 crackles.

Coconut Macaroons

3 eggwhites
3½ tablespoons fructose
vanilla essence to flavour
2 cups coconut
2 tablespoons arrowroot

Beat the eggwhites until soft peaks form, then beat in the fructose gradually. Fold in the vanilla, then the coconut and arrowroot, using a spatula. Cover oven trays with greased greaseproof paper, place teaspoonfuls of mixture on the trays and bake for 30 minutes or until set in a 150°C (300°F) oven. Carefully lift off the paper with a spatula and cool macaroons on racks. Store in airtight containers or freeze. These macaroons have many uses: they never freeze completely hard, so can be used almost straight from the freezer to accompany ice-cream and other cold desserts, or crushed as a topping on sundaes. The same recipe can be used as a "pavlova" case (p. 188) and to make unusual after-dinner biscuits (see Coconut Macaroon Cigars, p. 188). Makes about 24 small macaroons.

Coconut Biscuits

180 g (6 oz) margarine
1 tablespoon fructose or honey
60 g (2 oz) brown-rice flour or potato flour
180 g (6 oz) ground oats
4 tablespoons arrowroot
½ teaspoon bicarbonate of soda
1 teaspoon cream of tartar
100 g (3 oz) coconut
1 lightly beaten 60 g (2 oz) egg or gelatine mixture (egg substitute)

Melt the margarine and add honey (if used). Sift flour, fructose, arrowroot, soda and cream of tartar and mix in the coconut. Stir in beaten egg and melted margarine and mix well. Roll into small balls, flatten slightly with a fork and place on a greased tray. Bake at 180°C (350°F) for about 15 minutes. Makes 30 biscuits.

Oatmeal Macaroons

2 eggwhites
pinch cream of tartar
1 cup rolled oats
½ cup coconut

Beat the eggwhites with the cream of tartar until stiff. Fold in oats and coconut, and place mixture in teaspoonfuls on a greased oven tray. Bake in a moderate oven at 180°C (350°F) for 10 minutes. These are very plain, almost savoury, macaroons. Makes 15 macaroons.

Fruit Cheese Drops

Original Recipe:	*Substitution Suggestions:*
1 cup cottage cheese	goat's-milk cottage cheese (p. 87) or soya cheese (p. 88)
1 teaspoon grated orange rind	lemon rind if allergic only to orange-citrus
1 cup rolled oats	adjust quantity according to other flour used (see recipe below)
1 cup self-raising flour	wholegrain flour sifted with ½ teaspoon bicarbonate of soda and 1 teaspoon cream of tartar
½ cup castor sugar	omit sweetener or use honey to taste or 1 dessertspoon fructose
½ cup chopped raisins	stewed, fresh apricots, well drained
125 g (4 oz) melted butter	milk-free margarine
2 tablespoons orange juice	liquid from the stewed fruit

Sieve the cottage cheese and add the rind, oats, flour, fructose (if used) and raisins. Stir in the melted margarine (with honey, if used) and juice or liquid. Place teaspoonfuls on a greased tray and bake in a 190°C (375°F) oven for 20 minutes. These are substantial biscuits and are good for school lunches. Makes about 24 biscuits.

Using some of the substitutions above, the following recipe was devised:

Fruit Cheese Squares

  1 cup goat's cottage cheese
  1 teaspoon grated orange rind
  1½ cups rolled oats
  1 cup ground oats
  ½ teaspoon bicarbonate of soda
  1 teaspoon cream of tartar
  1 dessertspoon fructose or honey to taste
  ½ cup well-drained stewed apricots
  125 g (4 oz) melted margarine
  2 tablespoons orange juice

Sieve the cottage cheese and add the rind, oats, soda, cream of tartar, fructose or honey, and the apricots. Stir in the melted margarine and the juice. Place mixture in a slab tin, 18 by 28 cm (7 by 11 inches), and cook for about 25-30 minutes. Cut into squares.

Lincoln Crisps

3 eggwhites
pinch cream of tartar
1 teaspoon vanilla essence
2 level tablespoons melted margarine
²/₃ cup coconut
4 dessertspoons fructose
5 dessertspoons arrowroot
1 cup toasted soya beans or raw peanuts
4 cups toasted muesli (Mixed-grain or Whole-rice Muesli, see pp. 66-67)

Beat the eggwhites with the cream of tartar until stiff; add vanilla and margarine and beat again. Stir in other ingredients and, pressing mixture together with fingertips, form into buttons and place on a greased tray, or place in paper cases. Cook in a moderate oven, 180°C (350°F), for about 10-15 minutes or until slightly golden. Remove carefully from the tray with a spatula. Store in airtight containers. Makes about 20 biscuits.

Eggless Biscuits

3 medium bananas
⅓ cup oil
1 cup chopped dates (only ¼ cup, if hypoglycaemic)
½ cup chopped walnuts
2 cups rolled oats or flaked rice
1 teaspoon pure vanilla essence
1 teaspoon cinnamon

Mash the bananas and beat in the oil and dates. Add walnuts, oats, vanilla and cinnamon and mix. Allow to stand for 30 minutes until the oatmeal absorbs moisture. Drop in teaspoonfuls onto a greased oven tray and bake for 25 minutes in a moderate oven, 180°C (350°F). Take care with the cooking, as these biscuits burn easily. Makes about 40 biscuits.

Bran Macaroons

Original Recipe:	Substitution Suggestions:
4½ tablespoons margarine	4½ tablespoons margarine
1 dessertspoon fructose or 1 tablespoon honey	1 dessertspoon fructose or 1 tablespoon honey
2 well-beaten eggs	egg powder plus 2 table-spoons goat's or soya milk
3 cups wheat bran	3 cups rolled oats or other rolled grain
½ cup soya grits or chopped nuts (optional)	½ cup soya grits or chopped nuts (optional)
½ cup coconut (optional)	½ cup coconut (optional)
2 tablespoons wholewheat flour	2 tablespoons potato flour or rice bran or arrowroot
¼ teaspoon powdered allspice	1½ teaspoons powdered allspice
¼ teaspoon powdered ginger	1 teaspoon powdered ginger

Cream the margarine and sweetener, then add the eggs, mixing well. Add bran or rolled grain, and soya grits and coconut (if used). Sift flour with spices and add to the bran mixture; mix well. Place teaspoonfuls on a greased oven tray and bake in a 200°C (400°F) oven for 10-12 minutes. Makes 36 macaroons.

Oat Biscuits

125 g (4 oz) margarine
1 dessertspoon fructose or honey (optional)
1 teaspoon vanilla essence
2 eggs, separated
½ cup dried fruit (sultanas, currants, chopped raisins or apricots)
180 g (6 oz) rolled oats

OR

Rolled-rice Biscuits

125 g (4 oz) margarine
1 dessertspoon fructose or honey (optional)
1 teaspoon vanilla essence
2 eggs, separated, plus 1 white
½ cup dried fruit (sultanas, currants, chopped raisins or apricots)
2½ cups rolled rice or rice flakes, softened in boiling water

Cream the margarine and fructose (or honey, if used); add the egg yolks and beat well. Mix in the vanilla, dried fruit and oats or rice. Fold in the stiffly beaten eggwhites. Allow mixture to stand for 10 minutes. Place teaspoonfuls (pressing mixture together with fingertips, if necessary) close together on a greased oven sheet and bake at 200°C (400°F) for 15 minutes. Makes about 30 biscuits.

Cinnamon Biscuits

5 tablespoons margarine
1 dessertspoon fructose or 1 tablespoon honey or 1 tablespoon sultanas
1 cup flour (wheat or oatmeal or potato and rye or soya and arrowroot or rice flours, etcetera)
½ teaspoon bicarbonate of soda
1 teaspoon cream of tartar
1-2 teaspoons cinnamon (depending on flour used)
1-1½ teaspoons vanilla essence (depending on flour used)
1 tablespoon goat's or soya milk
extra 2 tablespoons milk (to liquefy sultanas, if used)

Cream the margarine with the fructose or honey (if used). Sift the flour, soda, cream of tartar and cinnamon and mix in well. Add vanilla and milk mixed together, and stir well. Place teaspoonfuls on a greased tray and bake at 190°C (375°F) for 15 minutes. Makes 18 biscuits.

Note: A good rice-flour combination is:
⅓ *cup brown-rice flour*
⅓ *cup arrowroot*
⅓ *cup rice bran*

Refrigerator Biscuits

250 g (8 oz) margarine
1 tablespoon fructose (optional)
2 eggs
2½ cups rye flour
1 cup potato flour
4 tablespoons arrowroot
1 teaspoon bicarbonate of soda
2 teaspoons cream of tartar
½ cup finely chopped nuts
½ cup finely chopped dates

Cream the margarine and add the fructose, blending well; add the eggs and beat well. Sift the dry ingredients together and mix in, then add the nuts and dates. Divide dough into two parts, shape into rolls and chill in the refrigerator overnight. Slice thinly for baking, place on a greased oven tray and bake at 190°C (375°F) for 7-10 minutes. The quantities may be halved, if appropriate. Makes 48 biscuits.

11
CAKES AND
SLICES

Again, in this chapter the emphasis is on how to use non-wheat flours, but wheat flour may be substituted if it is not an allergy food for you. Some general guidelines are:

• Refer to the section on the characteristics of the different flours in Chapter 7, p. 69, before you select the ones to use. Combinations you can rely on to work are rye-oat, rye-soya (a sticky one), soya-oat, soya-rice and wholly rice, so choose from these if you feel unsure of devising your own. Combinations with oats are best for biscuits rather than cakes. Other possible substitutes for 1 cup (4 oz) wheat flour are:

{ ½ cup cornflour or arrowroot
  ½ cup soya flour

{ ½ cup rye flour
  ½ cup potato flour

{ ¼ cup brown-rice flour
  ¼ cup potato flour
  ½ cup soya flour

{ ¼ cup brown-rice flour
  ¼ cup arrowroot
  ½ cup rice bran

• Cornflour, when used alone in fairly large amounts, as in scones, needs about the same amount of liquid as wheat flour, but the dough may spread and the product is crunchy and granular. If used in recipes which require only a small amount, cornflour can work quite well.
• When substituting wholewheat flour for white flour, simply double the rising agent—baking powder and/or eggs, baking

soda and cream of tartar. Two tablespoons of milk could be used in place of an extra egg.

• When soya flour is used, use only full-fat soya flour, not defatted. Soya flour is best used in combination with a dessertspoon or so at least of another flour. (I prefer considerably more other flour in proportion to the soya flour.) Vanilla essence goes well with soya flour and is a recommended addition if no juice or other flavouring is used.

• To make self-raising flour using plain flour, for every cup of flour sift through ½ teaspoon of bicarbonate of soda and 1 teaspoon of cream of tartar. More cream of tartar is necessary to neutralise the soda (see "Ingredients": "Bicarbonate of Soda", p. 13).

• Alternatively, well-soured milk or yoghurt may be used instead of the cream of tartar when soda is used (or as well as), since it is better to have the final product slightly acid than alkali. One cup of well-soured milk is needed for every ½ teaspoon of soda. Commercial sour milk, which has been stored, may have too high a yeast content for some, so make your own *when* you need it. To make 1 cup of sour milk from fresh milk, add 1¼ teaspoons of cream of tartar. Alternatively, use 1 tablespoon of lemon juice (not vinegar because of the yeast content) and enough milk to fill the 1-cup measure. One cup of fully soured milk plus ½ teaspoon soda equals 2 teaspoons of baking powder. If the sour milk plus soda is not sufficient, add (sifted with the dry ingredients) more soda and cream of tartar, or an egg if possible.

• Since no cane sugar is used, look for recipes that have fruit (and hence natural sweetness) in them, either fresh, frozen, lightly stewed or dried or use the tinned varieties in their natural juices. Apples, bananas and apricots are particularly good in cakes; peaches have a less definite flavour than apricots, and fresh cherries used in a plain pale cake make the surrounding cake mixture turn grey! Fresh cherries, however, are excellent in boiled fruit cakes, Christmas cakes and puddings.

When using dried fruit, buy unsulphured natural dried fruit (from health-food stores). All dried fruit should be rinsed thoroughly to clean and remove any excess sugar before using.

If using fruit in a recipe, then added sweeteners—fructose or honey—may be kept to a minimum. Again, it will be a matter of getting used to the less-sweet product at first.

• Some slices are easier to handle if chilled well first, and, since most of the slices and cakes have fruit in them, often the best place to keep them, for both reasons, is in the refrigerator. A few even take well to being used straight from the freezer; see Freezer Slice, p. 152, and Hedgehog Slice, p. 153.

• The perfect answer to the problem of an icing is to make an upside-down cake so that the swirl of sliced or halved fruit becomes the attractive topping; see the recipes for Apple Gingerbread on p. 128, and Banana Upside-down Cake, p. 132. Nuts, too, may be placed decoratively on the top of a cake before baking or in an upside-down fashion.

I find a spring-form tin is particularly useful for upside-down cakes. Remove the side piece and invert the cake over a plate or cooling rack so that the bottom may be gently and gradually lifted off the cake, and any fruit topping sticking to the bottom may be put back into its place on the cake very easily.

• For available sweeteners for use in baked products see the notes in the introduction to Chapter 10, p. 113. Refer to these notes if you are unsure about how to add the type of sweetener you choose in the following recipes. Fructose is added as you would add sugar, mostly creamed with the margarine. Obviously some recipes will have no milk or other liquid ingredient with which to blend sultanas, so this form of sweetener will not work, and recipes with a firm pastry base may not be suited to honey substitution, so some discretion is needed.

• Some recipes are already egg-free; to adapt the others consult the egg-substitute recipes given on pp. 15 and 16.

• As indicated in some of the recipes, if neither goat's nor soya milk are tolerated, substitute an appropriate fresh unsweetened fruit juice. Yoghurt may also be used if it is tolerated.

For the first recipe, I have given the original recipe (by permission of *Family Circle*), and then the modified version.

Note how much fruit (for natural sweetness) and spice (for flavour to go with non-wheat flours) there is in the original recipe, and hence why it was a good one to attempt to modify. Very plain cakes are not always successful when modified.

Prune Walnut Cake

½ cup butter
2 teaspoons grated orange rind

1 cup castor sugar

1 50 g egg
2 egg yolks
1 cup chopped stoned prunes
2 cups plain flour

1 teaspoon bicarbonate of soda

2 teaspoons baking powder

1 teaspoon cinnamon
good pinch salt
½ teaspoon nutmeg
¼ teaspoon allspice
½ cup buttermilk

½ cup chopped walnuts

Allergy Prune Walnut Cake

½ cup margarine
1 teaspoon grated orange rind (less because less sweetener is used)

1 tablespoon fructose or honey or ⅓ cup sultanas blended with the soured milk

{ 2 50 g eggs } or egg
{ 2 egg yolks } powder
1 cup chopped stoned prunes
{ 1 cup rice bran
{ 1 cup brown-rice flour

{ 1½ teaspoons bicarbonate of soda
{ 3 teaspoons cream of tartar
omit baking powder

1 teaspoon cinnamon
omit salt
½ teaspoon nutmeg
¼ teaspoon allspice
{ ½-¾ cup goat's) or ½-¾
{ or soya milk { cup orange
{ 1 tablespoon) juice
{ lemon juice
½ cup chopped walnuts

Add the lemon juice to the goat's milk or soya milk (if used)

126

and set aside. Cream the margarine, orange rind and fructose or honey. Add eggs and egg yolks, beating well, then stir in the well-rinsed prunes. Sift and mix in the dry ingredients alternately with the soured milk or orange juice; stir in the walnuts. Bake in two greased 20 cm (8 in) sandwich tins in a 160°C (325°F) oven for 35-40 minutes. Leave cakes for five minutes before turning out of the tins. When cold, join together with one of the icings or creams in Chapter 12. Dust the top with sifted arrowroot for effect only or cover with more icing or cream. As a variation, try baking the prepared mixture in a slab tin and cut it into squares for a slice or a dessert served with custard or ice-cream.

Passionfruit Apple Shortcake

125 g (4 oz) margarine
1 tablespoon fructose or honey
1 egg or gelatine mixture
1 cup rice bran
1 cup brown-rice flour
1 teaspoon bicarbonate of soda
2 teaspoons cream of tartar
2 peeled coarsely grated medium-sized apples
1 large or 2 small sliced bananas
pulp of 1 good-sized passionfruit
grated rind of 1 lemon
1½ tablespoons water

Cream the margarine and sweetener; add the egg and beat well. Mix in sifted flours, bicarbonate of soda and cream of tartar. Halve the mixture and press one half into the base of a 20 cm (8 in) greased sandwich tin. Cover with the apple, banana and passionfruit, then sprinkle over the lemon rind and the water. Roll out remaining half of dough onto greaseproof paper, invert over fruit to cover it, and peel off the paper. Press dough down well at the sides and brush top with water. Bake in a moderate oven, 180°C (350°F), for 35-40 minutes. This cake has an unusual fruity tang.

Upside-down Apple Gingerbread

Topping:
>   60 g (2 oz) margarine
>   1 tablespoon fructose
>   2 apples

Cake:
>   125 g (4 oz) margarine
>   1 dessertspoon fructose or honey
>   grated rind and juice of 1 lemon
>   2 eggs
>   ½ cup rice bran
>   ½ cup brown-rice flour
>   1½ teaspoons ground ginger
>   ½ teaspoon nutmeg
>   ½ teaspoon bicarbonate of soda
>   1 teaspoon cream of tartar

To prepare the topping, cream the margarine with the fructose until a light mixture is formed. Spread on base of a greased 20 cm (8 in) spring-form tin. Peel, quarter and slice the apples and arrange in a whirl over the base.

To prepare the cake, cream the margarine, fructose or honey (if used) and lemon rind until light and fluffy, gradually adding the lemon juice. Add the eggs singly, beating well, and fold in the sifted dry ingredients. Spread mixture gently over the apples in the tin and bake in a moderate oven, 180°C (350°F), for 35-45 minutes. Leave cake a few minutes in the tin before turning out. Serve as a cake or as a dessert with custard or ice-cream.

Allergy Apple Tea Cake

1 tablespoon margarine
1 dessertspoon fructose or 1 tablespoon honey or 2 tablespoons
   sultanas liquefied in the milk or juice
2 eggs
1-2 teaspoons vanilla essence
½ cup brown-rice flour
½ cup rice bran
½ teaspoon bicarbonate of soda
1 teaspoon cream of tartar
1 cup goat's or soya milk or unsweetened apple juice
1 grated apple
cinnamon

Cream the margarine and fructose until light and fluffy. Add
eggs and vanilla essence to taste, beating well. Add sifted dry
ingredients alternately with the milk, mixing evenly and
quickly. Place the mixture in a greased 18 cm (7 in) sandwich
tin, lined with greaseproof paper on the bottom. Cover with
grated apple and sprinkle with cinnamon, then bake in a
moderately hot oven, 190°C (375°F), for 40 minutes. Serve
fresh and sliced into wedges and spread with margarine or mock
cream (see Chapter 12).

Apricot Fruit Cake

60 g (2 oz) dried chopped apricots, unsulphured
60 g (2 oz) sultanas
1 medium grated carrot
½ cup water
2½ cups flour (any allowable, except all rye or all soya)
2 teaspoons cream of tartar
1 teaspoon bicarbonate of soda
75 g (2½ oz) sliced brazil nuts
¾ cup goat's or soya milk or fresh orange juice or unsweetened
   pineapple juice

Boil the first four ingredients together gently for five minutes.

Then add, sifted first, the remaining ingredients.

Mix the combined ingredients well, and turn into a 20 cm (8 in) cake tin, well greased and lined on the bottom with greased greaseproof paper. Bake in a moderate oven at 180°C (350°F) for 1¼-1½ hours. The end product is a light-coloured fruit cake.

Boiled Fruit Cake

1 cup raisins
1 cup sultanas
1 cup currants
1 cup water
250 g (8 oz) margarine
1½ teaspoons mixed spice
1 level teaspoon bicarbonate of soda
2 eggs
2 cups flour (any allowable, except all rye or all soya)
extra ½ teaspoon bicarbonate of soda
2 teaspoons cream of tartar

Put the dried fruit, water, margarine and spice into a saucepan, bring slowly to the boil then add the teaspoon of soda. Allow to cool slightly, then add the eggs, one at a time and unbeaten; mix well. Sift the flour with the ½ teaspoon of soda and cream of tartar and add to the fruit mixture. Turn into a 20 cm (8 in) round cake tin, lined on the bottom with greased greaseproof paper. Bake at 180°C (350°F) for 1½ hours. This is a darker-coloured fruit cake.

Basic Banana Loaf

This loaf is possible using many different flours or combinations of flours. There are three different combinations given here:

125 g (4 oz) margarine
1½ cups mashed banana
1 egg or *gelatine mixture*

1½ cups flour, e.g.:
  1½ cups rye flour
  or
  1 cup soya flour
  ½ cup brown-rice flour
  1 tablespoon rice bran
  or
  1 cup rice bran
  ¼ cup brown-rice flour
  ¼ cup arrowroot

¾ teaspoon bicarbonate of soda
1½ teaspoons cream of tartar
¼-⅓ cup goat's milk or *goat's yoghurt* or *soya milk* or *orange juice*

Cream the margarine, add the banana and beat with the margarine. Beat in the egg, then add flour(s), sifted with soda and cream of tartar, alternately with the liquid. Put in a 23 by 12 cm (9 by 5 in) loaf tin, greased and lined on the bottom with greased greaseproof paper.

If using rye flour, either place the loaf tin in a water-bath in the oven and bake at 180°C (350°F) for about 1½ hours; *or* place filled loaf tin in a microwave oven and bake on a medium heat for 20 minutes.

If using flour other than rye flour, bake loaf in a 180°C (350°F) oven for about one hour. Regardless of flour used, leave the cooked cake in the tin for 10 minutes before turning out. Cool, slice and spread with margarine to serve. Any tendency for the loaf to sink in the middle may be due to too many bananas in the mixture. This cake freezes well.

Banana Date Loaf

Vary the Basic Banana Loaf recipe by adding 2 teaspoons of lemon juice with milk, if used (not if orange juice is used), and ¾ cup chopped dates.

Banana Nut Loaf

Choose milk as the liquid—goat's or soya in this variation of the Basic Banana Loaf—mixed with 2 teaspoons of lemon juice to sour it. Add 1 teaspoon of vanilla essence with the egg and ²/₃ cup chopped nuts added last.

Banana Upside-down Cake

Topping:
>   1 dessertspoon fructose
>   60 g (2 oz) margarine
>   1 teaspoon cinnamon
>   4 or more bananas, sliced in half lengthways
>   juice ½ a lemon

Cake:
>   60 g (2 oz) margarine
>   1 dessertspoon fructose or 1 tablespoon honey or 2 tablespoons sultanas liquefied in the milk or juice (see below)
>   ½ cup coconut
>   1 egg
>   300 g (9 oz) flour, e.g.:

1 cup buckwheat flour		1 cup rice bran
½ cup brown-rice flour	or	½ cup brown-rice flour
½ cup potato flour		¼ cup arrowroot

>   1 teaspoon bicarbonate of soda
>   2 teaspoons cream of tartar
>   1½ teaspoons cinnamon
>   1 cup goat's or soya milk, or *unsweetened apricot juice*

Preheat the oven to 180°C (350°F). To make the topping, cream together the fructose, margarine and cinnamon.

Spread this mixture over the bottom of the cake tin, dip banana slices in lemon juice and arrange in a swirl over the topping, with the cut side of the bananas facing down.

To prepare the cake mixture, cream the margarine, add the fructose (or honey) and coconut and mix well. Add the egg and beat thoroughly. Sift together the flour, soda, cream of tartar and cinnamon and mix into the creamed mixture alternately with the milk or juice. Spread the mixture over the prepared topping in the tin and bake for one hour at 180°C (350°F). Invert onto a plate and leave a few minutes to set before removing the tin.

An egg-free variation can be made by replacing the egg with one mashed banana mixed with 2 tablespoons of extra liquid, *or* use the gelatine mixture (see recipe on p. 16), *or* add 1 teaspoon of baking powder in place of the egg.

Carrot Cake

2 large eggs
½ cup oil
2 tablespoons honey (or to taste) or 1 dessertspoon fructose or
⅓ cup sultanas liquefied in the milk/yoghurt
½ cup goat's yoghurt or ½ cup goat's or soya milk each with
1 dessertspoon lemon juice added or ½ cup fresh orange juice
2 cups flour, e.g. { 1 cup rice bran
{ 1 cup brown-rice flour
(for other possibilities see next recipe)
1 teaspoon bicarbonate of soda
2 teaspoons cream of tartar
1½-2 teaspoons cinnamon
1 cup grated carrot
1 cup coconut (optional)

Beat the eggs in a large bowl till frothy; add oil, sweetener and yoghurt or milk or juice and mix well. Add the flour, sifted with the soda, cream of tartar and cinnamon and mix thoroughly. Finally, add carrots and coconut (if used) and mix in. Bake in a greased 23 cm (9 in) ring tin in an oven preheated to

180°C (350°F) for about 45 minutes.

When I first began making this cake for my family a good 10 years ago, the thought of carrot being used in a cake was very odd to many people. Now carrot cakes are widely accepted and enjoyed because of their moistness and delicious flavour. On the same topic, check the Golden Fruit Pudding recipe in Chapter 13, p. 159. It has as much grated carrot by weight as flour, yet is a favourite with my family and friends.

Pumpkin Cake

> 2 large eggs
> ½ cup oil
> 1-2 tablespoons honey (or to taste) or 1 dessertspoon fructose or
> ⅓ cup sultanas liquefied in the milk/yoghurt
> ½ cup goat's yoghurt or goat's or soya milk, with 1 dessert-
> spoon lemon juice added
> 1 teaspoon vanilla essence
> 2 cups flour, e.g.:
> ¾ cup soya flour
> ½ cup brown-rice flour } or { 1 cup soya flour
> ¾ cup rice bran   1 cup fine oatmeal
> 1 teaspoon bicarbonate of soda
> 2 teaspoons cream of tartar
> 1 cup mashed cooked pumpkin
> ½ cup sultanas (if sultanas are used as sweetener, you may wish
> to decrease the number in the cake)

Beat the eggs in a large bowl till frothy; add the oil, sweetener, milk or yoghurt or juice, and vanilla. Then add the flour, sifted together with the soda and cream of tartar, and mix thoroughly. Fold in the mashed pumpkin and the extra sultanas. Bake in a greased 23 cm (9 in) ring tin in an oven preheated to 180°C (350°F) for about 45 minutes.

Allergy Granny Bun

60 g (2 oz) margarine
2 cups flour, e.g. ⎧ 1 cup rice bran
             ⎨ ½ cup brown-rice flour
             ⎩ ½ cup soya flour
1 teaspoon bicarbonate of soda
2 teaspoons cream of tartar
¾ teaspoon ground (or freshly grated) nutmeg
1 dessertspoon fructose or 1 tablespoon honey or ⅓ cup sultanas
    liquefied in the milk or omit sweetener altogether
2 handfuls dried fruit (sultanas, currants, raisins)
1 cup goat's or soya milk

Rub the margarine into the flour sifted with the soda, cream of
tartar and nutmeg. Add fructose (if used) and mix in. If using
honey, warm it slightly and stir into the milk before adding to
the flour mixture. Add dried fruit to flour mixture and then
add milk, mixing well. Turn into a well-greased and lined
23 by 12 cm (9 by 5 in) loaf tin and bake in moderate oven,
180°C (350°F), for about 1½ hours. Cool before slicing so it is
easier to cut, and serve buttered.

A dear friend who lived on a dairy farm in Victoria first
introduced our family to the basic Granny Bun. It is simple and
quick to mix, yet is always a popular loaf. It can also be served
sliced and toasted (if not all is eaten at the first sitting) and then
spread with margarine as a form of raisin toast—even at
breakfast-time.

Wholegrain Damper

1 cup unprocessed bran
1 cup rye flour
1½ cups wholemeal flour
¾ cup coconut
375 g (12 oz) raisins
1 teaspoon mixed spice
1¾ cups water

Wheat-free Variation

1 cup rice bran
1 cup rye flour
1½ cups fine oatmeal or soya flour
¾ cup coconut
375 g (12 oz) raisins
1½ teaspoons mixed spice
1¾ cups water

Mix all the ingredients together and shape into two damper-shaped loaves with your floured fingers. Place on a scone tray and bake at 200°C (400°F) for about 45 minutes. Serve warm if possible, sliced and buttered. Left-overs are delicious toasted like raisin bread.

Nectarine Coconut Cake

2 large eggs
½ cup oil
2 tablespoons honey or 1 tablespoon fructose
1 teaspoon vanilla essence
¾ cup goat's yoghurt or ¾ cup goat's or soya milk plus 1 tablespoon lemon juice added
2 cups flour, e.g. 1 cup each of rice bran and brown-rice flour or wholemeal (soya, rye and buckwheat flours may overpower the subtle flavour so are best left out of this recipe)
1 teaspoon bicarbonate of soda
2 teaspoons cream of tartar
1 cup coconut
1½ cups (or more) of nectarine slices (depending on thickness of slice)
3 teaspoons cinnamon (optional)

Beat the eggs and add oil, sweetener, vanilla and yoghurt or milk, mixing well. Stir in the flour sifted with the soda and cream of tartar. Add coconut and mix together. Grease a six-cup ring tin (preferably spring-form) and place a layer of cake mixture in the bottom of the tin, followed by a layer of fruit slices; sprinkle with cinnamon and then repeat layers until fruit and cake mixture are finished ending with cake mixture. Bake at 160°C (325°F) for 40-45 minutes.

This is an unusual fruity cake with an interesting delicate flavour—a summer treat. It can also be made with peaches, apples or strawberries instead of nectarines.

Small Cakes

Again I have begun this section by reprinting a delicious recipe (by permission of *Family Circle*) and then showing what these little cakes became.

Apple Cakes

½ cup sugar
1 egg
grated rind 1 lemon
1½ cups self-raising flour
90 g (3 oz) melted butter
  or margarine
3 tablespoons milk
  (allowable)
2 teaspoons lemon juice
½ cup cooked well-
  drained sweetened apple
1 teaspoon cinnamon
2 teaspoons sugar

Sugar-free Variation

2 eggs
grated rind 1 lemon
2¼ cups wholemeal plain
  flour
1 teaspoon bicarbonate of
  soda
2 teaspoons cream of
  tartar
juice ½ lemon
6 tablespoons unsweetened
  pineapple juice
4 tablespoons milk
  (allowable)
100 g (3 oz) melted
  margarine
1½ cups or more stewed
  apple pulp or other
  stewed fruit
cinnamon

Place the eggs and rind in bowl and add half the flour sifted with the soda and cream of tartar; make a well in the centre and add the mixed juices, milk and margarine. Beat with a wooden spoon for three minutes and add remaining flour. Spoon the mixture into patty cases so they are half full, add the fruit pulp and then top with more mixture. Sprinkle with cinnamon if desired. Bake in a moderately hot oven, 190°C (375°F), for 15 minutes. To serve, the cakes may be split and "cream" added to dress them up. Makes 12-15 cakes.

Note the decreased proportion of lemon juice and rind, as less is needed when the sugar is omitted; and the decrease in margarine but addition of fruit juice for sweetness. Other flours may be substituted if they are tolerated, such as soya or brown-rice flour with some oatmeal or potato flour mixed in too. Wholly brown rice flour and rice bran may be used too.

On a day when time was short and a dessert slice was needed, the little apple cakes became:

Apple Slice

2 eggs
rind 1 lemon
2½ cups tolerated flour
1 teaspoon bicarbonate of soda
2 teaspoons cream of tartar
juice 1 lemon
2¼ cups goat's or soya milk
100 g (3 oz) oil or melted margarine
1-1½ cups stewed apple
cinnamon

Place the eggs and rind in a bowl and add half the flour sifted with the soda and cream of tartar; make a well in the centre and add the mixed juice, milk and margarine or oil. Beat with a wooden spoon for three minutes and add the remaining flour. Spread half the batter over the base of an 18 by 28 cm (7 by 11 in) tin and spread the apple pulp over the top. Spoon the remaining batter over the apple and sprinkle with cinnamon if desired. Bake in a 190°C (375°F) oven for 25-30 minutes.

A few more changes produced the following "pudding". I have reproduced it here to give you some ideas about other ways you may use your cake recipes.

Apple Cake Pudding

125 g (4 oz) margarine
1 egg
1 teaspoon vanilla essence (no lemon this time)
*enough apple juice (unsweetened tinned or freshly juiced) for a
    soft spoonable consistency, or water*
2 cups flour
1 teaspoon bicarbonate of soda
2 teaspoons cream of tartar
¼ cup soya milk powder
stewed well-drained apple pulp
1 teaspoon mixed spice

Cream the margarine until light, then add the egg and vanilla essence and beat well. Add, alternately with the juice, the flour sifted with the soda, cream of tartar and soya milk powder. Spoon half the cake mixture over the base of a greased 18 by 28 cm (7 by 11 in) tin and spread the apple pulp over the top. Sprinkle with mixed spice. Spread the remaining cake mixture over the top and sprinkle with more mixed spice. Bake in a 190°C (375°F) oven for 25-30 minutes. Serves 6-8.

Modifications aside, other small cakes are:

Nutty Muffins

1 cup flour, e.g. rye, arrowroot, potato flour or soya
½ teaspoon bicarbonate of soda
1 teaspoon cream of tartar
¾ cup rice bran
⅓ cup chopped nuts
1 beaten egg
1 teaspoon vanilla essence
1 cup goat's or soya milk
1 dessertspoon fructose or 2 tablespoons sultanas or 1 tablespoon honey
60 g (2 oz) melted margarine

Preheat the oven to 200°C (400°F). Sift the flour, soda and cream of tartar, and add the bran and nuts; make a well in the centre of the dry ingredients. Mix the beaten egg, vanilla, milk and sweetener and add to the dry ingredients. Stir until blended only, but not necessarily smooth; add melted margarine and fold in. Spoon into greased patty tins or paper cases to three-quarters full and bake for about 25 minutes.

They may be served split and spread with margarine and Honey Caramel Sauce (recipe p. 46), if tolerated, or with stewed fruit, such as apple or apricots. Makes 24 small muffins.

Banana Muffins

2 beaten eggs
4 tablespoons melted margarine
1 teaspoon vanilla essence (optional, use if soya flour is used)
5 tablespoons goat's or soya milk, mixed with 3 teaspoons lemon juice or 5 tablespoons orange juice
2 cups mashed banana
2 cups flour
1 teaspoon bicarbonate of soda
2 teaspoons cream of tartar

Beat the eggs, margarine, vanilla, milk and bananas together. Add the sifted flour, soda and cream of tartar and mix only until no dry flour remains (the mixture may be lumpy). Spoon into greased patty tins or paper cases to three-quarters full. Bake for 35 minutes in a moderate oven at 180°C (350°F).

To serve, the muffins may be split and spread with margarine. Makes 20 small muffins.

Scones without Milk

1 dessertspoon melted margarine
1 cup pure fresh orange juice
2 cups flour, e.g. 1 cup soya and 1 cup brown-rice flour or 1 cup soya and 1 cup oatmeal or 1 cup rice bran, ½ cup arrowroot and ½ cup brown-rice flour
2 teaspoons cream of tartar plus 1 teaspoon bicarbonate of soda or 2 teaspoons corn-free baking powder

Mix the melted margarine with the juice and add to the flour sifted with the soda and cream of tartar. Mix lightly to form a soft dough. Cut into desired shapes with a floured cutter. Place on a greased and floured tray and bake in a very hot oven at 250°C (475°F) for 10 minutes. Makes about 8 scones.

For a variation add ½ cup of mashed cooked pumpkin and 2 tablespoons of sultanas.

Patty Cakes

100 g (3 oz) margarine
1 tablespoon fructose or honey or 2 tablespoons sultanas liquefied with the liquid
2 eggs
3-4 tablespoons goat's or soya milk or water
70 g (2¼ oz) brown-rice flour
70 g (2¼ oz) soya flour
2 teaspoons bicarbonate of soda
1 teaspoon cream of tartar
2 teaspoons vanilla essence

141

Cream the margarine and fructose or honey and add the eggs, beating well. Then add the milk or water alternately with the flour sifted with the soda and cream of tartar; finally, add the vanilla. Place mixture in well-greased patty tins or patty cases and bake in a hot oven at 200°C (400°F) for 10-15 minutes. Allow to cool and fill or decorate as desired (see Chapter 14, p. 196). Makes about 12 patty cakes.

You can vary this recipe in the following ways:

• Omit the sweetener and add one good-sized mashed banana, creaming it in with the margarine.
• Add ½ cup sultanas to the mixture.
• Omit milk or water and add fruit juice (freshly juiced or unsweetened tinned)—pineapple and orange are suitable. Decrease the sweetener or omit it altogether. Grated orange or lemon rind may also be creamed in with the margarine.
• Add 2-3 tablespoons of carob or cocoa to the basic mixture. When cool, top with a white topping (see Chapter 12) or simply dust with arrowroot.

Slices

Many slice recipes lend themselves well to adapting for allergy and sugar-free diets. If the cooked slice does not hold together well when cut while still warm, chill it well in the refrigerator first. Some slices will cut better the day after they are made.

Apricot Protein Slice

See Fruit Cheese Squares, p. 118.

Apricot Almond Slice

Short crust pastry (for an egg- and sugar-free pastry base, use that given in Crostata Slice, p. 151):

60 g (2 oz) ground oats ⎫ ⎧ *60 g (2 oz) brown-rice flour*
125 g (4 oz) soya flour ⎬ or ⎨ *125 g (4 oz) soya flour*
30 g (1 oz) potato flour ⎭ ⎩ *30 g (1 oz) rice bran*

    or ⎧ *100 g (3 oz) brown-rice flour*
       ⎩ *125 g (4 oz) soya flour*

1 tablespoon fructose
1 tablespoon arrowroot
125 g (4 oz) margarine
1 egg yolk
1 cup apricot jam (see recipe p. 92) or fresh or stewed, puréed apricots
1 eggwhite
1 tablespoon fructose
30 g (1 oz) ground almonds (blanched or unblanched)
1 tablespoon arrowroot
100 g (3 oz) chopped almonds (blanched or unblanched)

To prepare the pastry, mix flours, fructose and arrowroot evenly then rub in the margarine till blended. Add the egg yolk and mix to a dough. Alternatively, place all ingredients in a food processor bowl and process until a ball forms.

Roll or pat out the pastry to fit a 23 by 30 cm (9 by 12 in) baking tray with sides slightly raised to contain the mixture. Spread centre of pastry with the apricots or jam. Beat the eggwhite until stiff, add the fructose and beat again. Fold in ground almonds and arrowroot and spread this meringue mixture over the jam. Sprinkle generously with the chopped almonds. Bake in a moderate oven, 180°C (350°F), until pale brown—about 30 minutes. Preferably chill the slice or at least allow to cool thoroughly before slicing.

Note that this recipe is suitable only for those who can tolerate fructose.

Apricot Coconut Slice

    1 cup soya flour
    1 teaspoon bicarbonate of soda
    2 teaspoons cream of tartar
    1 cup coconut
    ½ cup sunflower (or other allowable) oil
    1 cup apricot liquid and goat's or soya milk mixed
    500 g (1 lb) apricots and liquid (fresh, halved and lightly stewed
        or tinned in natural juice only)

Sift the flour, soda and cream of tartar into a bowl and add the coconut. Make a well in the centre of the dry ingredients and add the oil and liquid mixed; stir well to mix. Fold apricot halves through the mixture and then turn the mixture into a slice tin, 18 by 28 cm (7 by 11 in). Bake in a moderate oven, 180°C (350°F), for 30-40 minutes until just golden.

Apple Crumble Slice

Filling:

    4 large peeled and sliced apples
    1 teaspoon cinnamon
    1 tablespoon margarine
    2 teaspoons lemon juice
    2 teaspoons water

Cake:

    1½ cups flour
    1 teaspoon bicarbonate of soda
    2 teaspoons cream of tartar
    1 tablespoon fructose or honey or 2 tablespoons sultanas liquefied
        with the liquid
    ¼ teaspoon ground cloves
    ⅓ cup melted margarine
    ⅓ cup milk, soya milk or apple juice (freshly juiced or
        unsweetened tinned)
    2 eggs
    ½ teaspoon vanilla essence

144

Crumb topping:
 60 g (2 oz) margarine
 ½ cup flour (brown-rice flour plus rice bran)
 1-2 teaspoons fructose or *honey (optional)*
 ½ cup chopped walnuts

To prepare the filling, place the apples in a saucepan with other ingredients, cover and simmer until apples are just tender. Cool and drain well.

To prepare the cake, sift the flour, soda, cream of tartar, fructose (if used) and cloves into a bowl. If honey is used, add to the margarine when melting. Add melted margarine (and honey if used), milk or juice, eggs and vanilla; beat well until blended. Spread half of the mixture in a well-greased slab tin, 20 by 30 cm (8 by 12 in) and cover with half the apples. Repeat cake and apple layers, finishing with an apple layer.

To prepare the topping, rub the margarine into the flour and fructose (if used) and add the walnuts; *or* cream the margarine and honey, add flour and mix till crumbly; add the walnuts. Sprinkle crumb topping over the apples and bake in a moderate oven, 180°C (350°F), for 35-40 minutes.

Spicy Apple Slice

Pastry (or use egg-free Crostata Slice pastry, p. 151):
 100 g (3 oz) margarine
 1 teaspoon fructose or *1 tablespoon sultanas liquefied with the egg yolk and water*
 1 egg yolk ⎱
 1-2 tablespoons water ⎰ *(mixed)*
 1½ cups flour (any allowable, except all rye)
 ¼ teaspoon bicarbonate of soda
 ½ teaspoon cream of tartar

Filling:

- *4 large peeled and thinly sliced apples*
- *2 tablespoons water*
- *a few cloves or pinch ground cloves*
- *a few strips lemon rind*
- *1 teaspoon margarine*

Topping:

- *¾ cup brown-rice flour*
- *1 tablespoon arrowroot*
- *4 teaspoons cinnamon*
- *2 teaspoons fructose (optional)*
- *2½ tablespoons margarine*

To prepare the pastry, cream the margarine and fructose (if used) until light, add the egg yolk and water mixture and beat well. Sift the flour, soda and cream of tartar and knead into a creamed mixture. Form into a ball and chill for half an hour. Roll out to fit a greased slab tin, 20 by 25 cm (8 by 10 in).

To prepare the filling, place apple slices in a saucepan with the water, cloves, lemon rind and margarine and simmer until apples are softened. Cool before placing in uncooked pastry shell.

To prepare the topping, sift the flour(s) and cinnamon into a bowl and add fructose (if used); rub in margarine. Shape into a ball, chill until firm and then grate coarsely over the apples. Bake the slice in a moderate oven, 180°C (350°F), for about 40 minutes.

Apple Walnut Bars

1 egg

1 dessertspoon fructose or honey or 2 tablespoons sultanas liquefied with stewed apples

¼ cup melted margarine

½ cup puréed stewed apples

1 cup flour, e.g. rye, potato and brown rice or rye and soya or brown rice and rice bran

½ teaspoon bicarbonate of soda

1 teaspoon cream of tartar

1 tablespoon cocoa or 2 tablespoons carob powder

½ teaspoon cinnamon

¼ teaspoon ground cloves

pinch nutmeg

½ cup chopped walnuts

Beat the egg until frothy and beat in the fructose (if used); stir in the margarine and puréed apples. Sift together the flour, soda, cream of tartar, cocoa or carob, cinnamon, cloves and nutmeg, and stir into the egg mixture; then add the walnuts. Turn into a greased 18 by 18 cm (7 by 7 in) slice tin and bake in a moderate oven, 180°C (350°F), for about 40 minutes. Cool the slice in the tin before slicing.

Spiced Rye Slice

125 g (4 oz) margarine
1 tablespoon fructose
1 egg
1 cup rye flour
½ cup soya flour
2 tablespoons potato flour
½ teaspoon cinnamon
¾ teaspoon ginger
¾ teaspoon bicarbonate of soda
1½ teaspoons cream of tartar
1½ cups stewed apple

Cream the margarine and fructose, then add the egg and beat well. Add the flours sifted with the cinnamon, ginger, soda and cream of tartar. Add apple pulp, mixing well. Turn into a 18 by 28 cm (7 by 11 in) slab tin and bake at 190°C (375°F) for 40-45 minutes.

Rye-fruit Slice

juice and rind of 1 lemon
1¼-1½ cups milk
125 g (4 oz) margarine
1 tablespoon fructose or honey or ½ cup sultanas liquefied in ½ cup of the milk
2 eggs
3 cups rye flour
1 teaspoon bicarbonate of soda
2 teaspoons cream of tartar
3 peeled and diced pears

Mix the lemon juice with the milk and set aside. Cream the margarine with the fructose or honey and lemon rind, then add the eggs, beating well. Add sifted flour, soda and cream of tartar alternately with the milk mixture. Lastly, fold in the diced pears. Bake in a microwave dish, 20 by 20 cm (8 inches square), in a microwave oven on medium-low for 25-30 minutes. Ideally, finish off with convection at 180°C (350°F) for 10 minutes.

Coffee Cake

1 tablespoon fructose
¾ cup margarine
¼ cup halved walnuts
3 cups flour, e.g.:

1½ cups soya flour
1½ cups brown-rice flour } or { 1 cup soya flour
1 cup oatmeal
½ cup brown-rice flour

1½ teaspoons bicarbonate of soda
3 teaspoons cream of tartar
⅔-1 cup goat's or soya milk
1 tablespoon lemon juice } (mixed)
1½ cups raw grated apple
1½ cups sliced banana
cinnamon

Mix the fructose and ¼ cup of margarine and spread over the bottom of a 23 cm (9 in) cake tin; press walnut halves into the mixture, forming a pattern. Sift together the flour, soda, cream of tartar and rub in the remaining margarine with your fingertips. Fold in the milk and juice mixture and form mixture into a soft dough. Roll out on greaseproof paper or a pastry sheet into an oblong, 50 by 25 cm (20 by 10 in). Arrange fruit on the dough and sprinkle generously with cinnamon. Roll up like a jam roll and cut the roll into 2½ cm (1 in) slices. Place the slices flat, close together, on the margarine in the tin and bake for about 45 minutes in a hot oven at 200°C (400°F) until golden. When cooked, turn out so the walnuts are uppermost. Serve warm, breaking each coffee cake off at the marked divisions.

These slices freeze well, and are delicious microwaved briefly to reheat.

Coconut Squares

½ cup margarine
1 cup coconut
1 cup flour (almost any except all rye)
½ teaspoon bicarbonate of soda
1 teaspoon cream of tartar
½ cup goat's or soya milk

For this very basic everyday slice that's quick to make, melt the margarine in a medium-sized saucepan, remove from the heat and add the coconut and the sifted flour, soda and cream of tartar alternately with the milk.

Variations on this basic slice are as follows:

• For a sweeter slice—1 tablespoon of fructose *or* honey added to the melted butter *or* ½ cup sultanas liquefied in a blender with the milk, and then add this mixture alternately with the flour.

• Omit sweeteners and add 1 tablespoon carob (*or* 1 dessert-spoon cocoa) plus 1 mashed banana mixed with the milk.

• Omit the milk and add fructose *or* honey and 1 teaspoon (or to taste) grated lemon *or* orange rind and ½ cup orange juice in place of the milk. If sultanas are used to sweeten the mixture, liquefy them in the orange juice.

Crostata Slice

Pastry:

>   1½ cups flour, e.g. ¾ cup soya flour and ¾ cup brown-rice flour
>   ¾ teaspoon bicarbonate of soda
>   1½ teaspoons cream of tartar
>   1 tablespoon sultanas or 2 teaspoons fructose
>   3 tablespoons margarine
>   3 tablespoons lemon juice

Filling:

>   3 medium peeled and sliced cooking apples
>   1 tablespoon margarine
>   500 g (1 lb) goat's cottage cheese
>   2 eggs
>   2 tablespoons brown-rice flour
>   2 teaspoons grated lemon rind
>   1 tablespoon sultanas or 2 teaspoons fructose
>   ½ cup goat's or soy milk
>   ½ cup raisins

To prepare the pastry, sift flour, soda and cream of tartar and add fructose (if used). Rub in the margarine. Liquefy the sultanas (if used) in the lemon juice, add to flour and knead into a stiff dough. Wrap and chill for half an hour.

To prepare the filling, simmer the apples and margarine together for one-two minutes. Beat, till thoroughly blended, the cottage cheese, eggs, flour, lemon rind, fructose and milk or sultanas liquefied in the milk.

Roll out the pastry to 3-6 mm (⅛-¼ in) thick to fit a 22 cm (9 in) square deep baking dish or tin, keeping any left-over pastry for strips for the top. Arrange the apples over the pastry. Sprinkle with half the raisins and spoon the cheese mixture over, then top with remaining raisins. Make strips 12 mm (½ in) wide from the remaining pastry, and form a lattice over the top; brush with water. Bake in a moderate oven, 180°C (350°F), for an hour or until set. Chill well before serving. The slice is like a "mini-cheesecake", suitable served as a cake or a dessert.

Freezer Slice

2 eggs
1 dessertspoon fructose
2 tablespoons arrowroot
1 cup coconut
½ cup each sultanas and chopped raisins (prepared by rinsing
   in boiling water)
½ cup chopped dried apricots
½ cup chopped walnuts

Beat the eggs and fructose until thick, then blend in the arrow-root, coconut, fruit and nuts. Spread mixture in a slice tin and bake in a 180°C (350°F) oven for 30-40 minutes. Cool in tin, cut into slices and chill thoroughly, although it may cut more easily if chilled first. The name of this grain-free slice arose from the discovery that it handles well straight from the freezer, as it never goes completely solid (like the Coconut Macaroon Cigars, p. 188). It is also easier to slice if frozen first; then simply store the pieces in the freezer. The same recipe is used in Santa's Buttons, p. 184.

Copha Slice

2 cups basic Whole-rice Muesli (p. 67)
1 dessertspoon fructose or honey (optional)
1 cup coconut
½ cup sultanas
½ cup chopped dried apricots
½ cup raisins
carob powder or cocoa (optional)
⅔ cup melted copha

Mix the muesli, fructose (if used), coconut and dried fruit in a bowl; add the carob or cocoa (if used) and mix. Add the honey (if used) to the copha, and pour it over the dry ingredients. Spread mixture in a slice tin (about 20 cm or 8 in square) or else spoon into paper cases; chill until set. Store in the refrigerator.

Hedgehog Slice

125 g (4 oz) margarine
3 teaspoons honey or 2 teaspoons fructose (optional)
3 tablespoons coconut
2 tablespoons carob or cocoa
1 beaten egg
1 tablespoon arrowroot
¾ cup chopped walnuts
250 g (8 oz) crushed sweet biscuits, e.g. Banana Oat Biscuits,
  p. 114; Cinnamon Biscuits, p. 121; Refrigerator Biscuits, p. 122

Place the margarine, sweetener (if used), coconut and carob in a saucepan and cook for two minutes. Cool slightly, then add the egg, arrowroot, walnuts and biscuits. Press firmly into a flat tin (20 cm or 8 in square). Chill well or store in, and serve from, the freezer for easy handling.

12
ICINGS AND
CREAMS

Without icing sugar or cream, traditional cake toppings may seem difficult to make. However, the following recipes will help on those occasions where an upside-down cake, which does not need icing, is not possible. The quantity produced by each recipe will be sufficient to fill or top a single cake or a batch of cup cakes.

Goat's Cheese Mock Cream

Goat's-milk Cottage Cheese (see recipe p. 87)
extra goat's milk
vanilla essence (optional)
fructose or *honey* or *Equal (optional)*

Beat the required amount of goat's cottage cheese until smooth. Gradually add small amounts of goat's milk until the desired consistency is reached, flavour with vanilla to taste and add fructose, Equal *or* honey only if necessary. Use as cake topping or filling (make a firmer cream for a filling) or on scones or pikelets in place of cream.

Dairy-free Mock Cream

125 g (4 oz) copha
1-2 tablespoons fructose
1 teaspoon vanilla
1 tablespoon hot water

Use copha that is at room temperature; chop it roughly (or grate) and place in a warmed basin with the fructose. Beat on medium speed with an electric mixer until light and fluffy; then beat in the vanilla and hot water. The cream will set firmly.

White Drizzle

1 tablespoon arrowroot
1 tablespoon fructose
¾ teaspoon gelatine
2 tablespoons cold goat's or soya milk
½ cup goat's or soya milk

Mix the arrowroot, fructose and gelatine with the cold milk, then add the ½ cup of milk and heat mixture until it is thick and the gelatine has dissolved. This recipe makes a "dripping" glaze to be spooned over large cakes. You will find that the glaze remains moist.

Custard Cream

2 teaspoons gelatine
1½ tablespoons boiling water
flavouring, e.g. vanilla essence or carob or cocoa or orange juice
1 cup thick custard (see recipe p. 46)

Dissolve the gelatine in the boiling water and add flavouring to custard. Combine the gelatine and flavoured custard and use when semi-set as a cake topping or filling.

Whipped Cream Substitute

1 eggwhite
1 mashed banana

Whip the eggwhite until stiff, then add the mashed banana and continue whipping until it is dissolved. This recipe makes a soft cream.

Broiled Icing

½ cup margarine
2 teaspoons fructose or 1 tablespoon honey
2 tablespoons goat's or soya milk or water (less if honey is used)
⅓ cup chopped nuts
¾ cup coconut

Melt the margarine in a pan, add the other ingredients and mix well. Spread the icing over cake, and place low under a griller and broil until the icing is bubbling—watch carefully as the coconut scorches easily. This icing is good for fairly plain cakes or spiced cakes without added fruit. The recipe makes enough for toppings for two 22 cm (9 in) round cakes. You can vary the icing by omitting the nuts and using 1 cup of coconut and adding ½ teaspoon of vanilla essence.

Chocolate or Carob Icing 1

3 teaspoons margarine
3 tablespoons melted copha
6 tablespoons carob powder or cocoa

Add the margarine to the copha, melt and stir till blended with the copha. Pour over carob or cocoa in a bowl or cup and mix well. Allow to cool a little, then pour on top of cake and spread evenly with a knife. Chill until the icing is set. This recipe makes a smooth, hard "real-chocolate"-type coating and it may be used on large or small cakes or over Coconut Macaroons (p. 116). The quantity given here is enough for one 20 cm (8 in) or 22 cm (9 in) cake.

Chocolate or Carob Icing 2

1 dessertspoon margarine
1 tablespoon arrowroot
1 tablespoon carob powder or 1 dessertspoon cocoa
2 teaspoons water
1 teaspoon fructose or honey to taste (decrease water if necessary)
   or Equal powder to taste

Mix all the ingredients together, beating well. This recipe makes a spreadable icing for large or small cakes and is enough for one 20 cm (8 in) cake top. Decorate with coconut, or chopped or whole nuts.

Banana Topping Cream

See recipe on p. 173. Any frozen fruit topping may be used in place of cream, on fresh fruit salad particularly.

Coconut Macaroon Covering

The Coconut Macaroon mixture (see recipe p. 116) may be spread to completely cover a birthday or other cake. The covered cake is then baked in a 160°C (325°F) oven for 15 minutes or until the macaroon is set—it produces a "roughed-up" icing effect. Do make sure the iced cake will fit back in the oven if using this covering!

Banana Apricot Filling

4 mashed bananas
4 tablespoons puréed apricots
1 tablespoon mandarine, orange or pineapple juice
¼ teaspoon vitamin C powder

Mix together the bananas and apricots and gradually add the juice until the desired consistency is reached. Add vitamin C powder to prevent the bananas turning brown. Use to fill large or small, plain cakes.

13
DESSERTS

Impossible Pie

4 eggs

*1 dessertspoon fructose or 1 tablespoon honey or ½ cup sultanas
liquefied in 1 cup of the milk*

½ cup flour (oatmeal, rice are good)

½ cup softened margarine

2 cups goat's or soya milk

1 teaspoon vanilla essence

1 cup coconut

Mix all the ingredients together—a food processor is excellent
here. Pour the mixture into a greased deep-sided oven dish and
bake till set in a moderate to slow oven, 160°C (325°F), for
about 45 minutes. The method may sound impossible but the
end result is a layered pudding, the flour forming a pudding
base with a creamy custard topped with coconut.

Golden Fruit Pudding

½ cup brown-rice flour ⎫
½ cup rice bran ⎬ *(or other flours to make 1 cup)*
½ teaspoon nutmeg
½ teaspoon bicarbonate of soda
1 teaspoon cream of tartar
1½ tablespoons margarine
1 cup dried fruit, e.g. ½ cup sultanas and ½ cup chopped raisins
1¼ cups tightly packed, coarsely grated carrot
2 teaspoons grated lemon rind ⎫
1 teaspoon grated orange rind ⎬ *(less if preferred)*
1 beaten egg
3 tablespoons goat's or *soya milk* or *orange juice* or *water*

Sift the dry ingredients into a bowl and rub in the margarine until the mixture resembles dry breadcrumbs; add dried fruit, carrot and rind. Mix the beaten egg with the chosen liquid and add to the dry ingredients. Place in a greased bowl, cover securely and steam in a saucepan of boiling water for 1½-2 hours. Serve with custard or other allowable "cream". This is an unusual but delicious steamed pudding, excellent for cold days or really hungry children. The carrot is good for added sweetness and moistness, not to mention the nutritional value. Serves 6.

Pineapple-baked Apples

This is our family's favourite way of baking apples and is popular with guests, too, despite the absence of any sugar or honey. The flavours complement each other beautifully.

Fill cored apples with chopped pineapple, fresh or unsweetened tinned, and top with chopped almonds. Pour over apples some unsweetened pineapple or apple juice or water and bake at 180°C (350°F) for 45 minutes. The juice will go toffee-like, and the almonds become toasted (watch for scorching). Serve with ice-cream or cream.

Apple Crumble

> 4 cups sliced apples, with or without skin (more if you prefer a
>   deep pie)
> 2 teaspoons lemon juice and water to make ½ cup
> 100 g (3 oz) margarine
> 1 cup flour (almost any except buckwheat or soya on its own)
> 1 tablespoon finely chopped sultanas or 1 dessertspoon fructose
> 1 teaspoon grated lemon rind
> 1-2 teaspoons cinnamon

This recipe is a variation on the long-time favourite. Instead of
first stewing the apple, try this: place apples in greased pie dish
and pour over the lemon juice and water mixed. Rub the
margarine into the flour and fructose (*or* chopped sultanas) until
it resembles breadcrumbs. Add the lemon rind and mix well.
Spread over the apples and sprinkle generously with cinnamon.
Bake in a 190°C (375°F) oven for about 40 minutes until the
apples are tender and the topping is crispy brown. Serves 4-6.

Fruit Crumble Topping Variations

-    2 cups rolled oats
     ¹/₈ cup coconut
     ¼ cup soya grits
     2 tablespoons margarine
     1 dessertspoon fructose
     cinnamon

-    ½ cup buckwheat
     ½ cup coconut
     2 tablespoons margarine
     1 teaspoon mixed spice
     2 teaspoons fructose

- ½ cup rice bran
  ½ cup brown-rice flour
  ½ cup coconut
  1½-2 tablespoons margarine
  1 teaspoon cinnamon

- In above variation, omit coconut and add about 25 g (1 oz) of coarsely chopped walnuts—particularly delicious with apples or pears. Watch carefully during baking as the walnuts may scorch.

For all variations: mix all ingredients together until the mixture is crumbly. Spread over fresh sliced fruit (Fruit Crisp) or stewed fruit (Fruit Crumble), and sprinkle generously with cinnamon. Apples, apricots, pears and rhubarb are all delicious stewed and served with a topping.

Pear and Date Crumble

750 g (1½ lb) pears
250 g (8 oz) fresh or dried dates
¼-½ teaspoon ground allspice
²/₃ cup orange juice

Peel, core and dice the pears. Halve and stone the dates and place with the pears, allspice and orange juice in an ovenproof dish. Sprinkle with the first topping variation on p. 160 (omit soya grits). Bake for 40 minutes at 180°C (350°F). Serves 6.

Apple Cake Pudding

The final adaptation of the little Apple Cakes recipe gives this pudding (see p. 137). If apples are not available, substitute fresh, lightly stewed apricots; drain them well but reserve the juice to use as liquid in the cake mixture.

Apple Rice Bake

60 g (2 oz) margarine
2 cups cooked brown rice
125 g (4 oz) chopped raisins
1 teaspoon cinnamon
2 cups stewed apples
breadcrumbs from allowable bread (optional)

Melt the margarine and stir in the rice and well-rinsed raisins. Add cinnamon to stewed apples and arrange in layers in a greased casserole dish. Top with breadcrumbs if desired. Bake for 20 minutes in a moderate oven at 180°C (350°F). Serve warm with custard (p. 46), ice-cream (p. 174) or junket. Serves 6.

A very similar recipe to Apple Rice Bake for those who cannot have dried fruit such as raisins is the following:

Winter Pudding

60 g (2 oz) melted margarine
1 cup or more cooked brown rice or *soft breadcrumbs of allowable bread*
3 large, sliced raw apples and 2 sliced bananas
1-2 teaspoons cinnamon or to taste

Melt sufficient margarine to coat the rice *or* breadcrumbs, then stir till well coated. Place alternate layers of rice and fruit, beginning with rice, in a greased casserole dish, and sprinkle the fruit layers with a little cinnamon; end with a layer of rice and dot with butter. Cover and bake for 40 minutes until the fruit is soft at 180°C (350°F). Uncover the dish towards the end if a crunchy top is preferred, and serve with ice-cream, custard or plain junket. Serves 6.

Spiced Apple Pie

1 quantity Dessert Tart Pastry (p. 108)
1 tablespoon brown-rice flour
1 teaspoon mixed spice
¼ teaspoon ground cloves
¼ teaspoon ground nutmeg
1 kg (2 lb) peeled and sliced Granny Smith apples
¼ cup well-rinsed sultanas
3 teaspoons grated lemon rind

Mix together the flour and spices. Place apple slices and sultanas in a large bowl and coat with the flour mixture. Turn the fruit into a deep-sided 20 cm (9 in) tart dish lined with the pastry, and sprinkle the lemon rind over the top, using an edging strip of pastry; make vent holes. Brush with water or milk and bake in a moderately hot oven at 190°C (375°F) for about 30-40 minutes or until the pastry is cooked and golden. Serve with custard, ice-cream or plain junket. Serves 6-8.

Almond Apple Soufflé

2 cups cooked apples
100 g (3 oz) margarine
1 tablespoon fructose or honey or ⅓ cup sultanas liquefied with the lemon juice
2 teaspoons grated lemon rind
1 tablespoon lemon juice
½ cup ground almonds
3 eggs, separated

Purée the apples and spoon them over the base of greased six-cup-size deep ovenproof dish. Beat together the margarine, fructose or honey and lemon rind until blended, then beat in juice (and sultanas if used), ground almonds and egg yolks. Fold in stiffly beaten eggwhites and spread the mixture over the apples. Bake in a moderate oven at 180°C (350°F) for 40-45 minutes or until the top is lightly browned and springs back when touched. Serve warm or cold, with ice-cream or custard if liked. This is an unusual grain-free soufflé dessert which is special enough to serve to guests. Serves 6.

Latticed Apple Slice

Pastry:

>125 g (4 oz) margarine
>1½ cups flour
>2 teaspoons fructose or 1 tablespoon sultanas
>1 beaten egg

Filling:

>6 large apples, e.g. cooking, Granny Smith's, new season's Golden Delicious
>3 tablespoons water
>few strips lemon rind
>2 tablespoons soft breadcrumbs from allowable bread
>60 g (2 oz) sultanas
>1 dessertspoon cinnamon

If using sultanas as sweetener, blend briefly on high speed with ½ cup of the flour till well chopped, then combine with the rest of the flour. Rub the margarine into the flour with your fingertips and add fructose (if used). Add beaten egg and mix to form a firm dough, reserving any excess beaten egg for final glazing. Chill for half an hour.

Peel and slice the apples and place them in a saucepan with the water and lemon rind. Simmer gently until apples are just softened, then allow to cool.

Roll out two-thirds of the pastry to fit a greased slab tin 25 by 20 cm (10 by 8 in), and sprinkle the breadcrumbs over the pastry. Spoon the cold apples over the pastry and sprinkle with the sultanas. Roll out remaining pastry, cut into strips and use to form a lattice over the fruit. Glaze with beaten egg (remaining from pastry) or milk or water and sprinkle generously with cinnamon. Bake in a moderate oven at 180°C (350°F) for about 45 minutes. Serve warm or cold. Serves 6.

Apple Custard Bake

4 large apples, e.g. cooking, Granny Smith's
¼ cup water
3 55 g eggs
2 cups goat's or soya milk
1½ teaspoons vanilla essence
2 dessertspoons fructose or 1 tablespoon honey (or to taste) or
   1 tablespoon sultanas liquefied in 1 cup of the milk
extra 1 tablespoon sultanas (if allowed)

Peel and slice the apples and cook gently in a saucepan with ¼ cup of water for seven minutes. Meanwhile, beat the eggs with the milk, vanilla and fructose or honey until blended. Place the drained apples in a baking dish, sprinkle over the extra sultanas (if used) and pour over the milk mixture. Set the dish in a larger pan of hot water and bake at 180°C (350°F) for 45 minutes or until the custard is set. Serve warm or cold. This is a simple dessert, complete by itself, which is very popular with children. Serves 4-6.

Crostata Slices

See Chapter 11, p. 151. As a dessert, serve in large squares with any allowed ice-cream or topping if desired. See Chapter 12 for toppings.

Baked Bananas

1-1½ bananas per person
1 teaspoon margarine per banana
cinnamon

Peel the bananas, slice lengthways and place in a greased casserole dish. Sprinkle generously with cinnamon and dot with the margarine. Bake in a moderate oven at 180°C (350°F) for about 20 minutes until bananas are just soft.

To this basic recipe add either of the following variations:

• For about six bananas: ½ cup fresh orange juice and 1 cup of coconut poured over before baking.

• Sprinkle sliced bananas with chopped nuts—walnuts, almonds, brazil nuts—as well as the cinnamon. Pour over ½ cup or so of fresh orange *or* mandarine juice. Dot with margarine and bake as above.

Pancakes

Once you have chosen a suitable pancake recipe (see Chapter 9, p. 97) then you are able to choose from an almost endless variety of fillings for a delicious and special dessert. I have given a few possibilities but many other cookbooks give them too. Most dessert pancake fillings include fruit of some sort so added sweeteners can often be omitted. Remember that you may need to decrease the amount of added lemon juice or other less-sweet fruit if sweeteners are omitted. A small amount of vitamin C powder (see Chapter 1, p. 24) dissolved in a little juice or water may be used to prevent browning of apples or bananas, instead of lemon juice. Remember, too, to use fresh or frozen fruit, or else preserved juice may be substituted for brandy or other spirits for marinating the fruit, or for use in a sauce.

Apple Sultana Filling

> *½ cup raisins or sultanas*
> *3 tablespoons fresh orange juice or pineapple juice*
> *2 cups diced peeled apple*
> *100 g (3 oz) margarine*
> *¼ cup finely chopped walnuts*

Soak the raisins or sultanas in the juice for at least one hour. Heat the apples gently in the margarine, stirring frequently, for 10 minutes until slightly softened. Add the walnuts and marinated dried fruit—spoon the mixture onto pancakes. Roll up pancakes and place, folded side down, in an ovenproof dish. Warm in a slow oven, 150°C (300°F), for 10-15 minutes and serve warm with ice-cream or allowable topping. This filling is sufficient for 8-12 pancakes.

Tropical Macaroon Filling

1 small fresh pineapple
4 tablespoons lightly stewed or puréed apricots
4 tablespoons lightly crushed Coconut Macaroons (see recipe p. 116)
2 tablespoons fresh orange or pineapple juice
1 tablespoon melted margarine

Remove the skin and core from the pineapple and chop the flesh finely. Mix with the apricots, heat in a saucepan and spread the warm filling over the pancakes. Sprinkle with crushed macaroons, then pour on the juice. Form into triangles by folding the pancakes in half, then in half again. Place in a greased ovenproof dish and brush with melted margarine. Heat in a hot oven, 220°C (425°F), for five minutes or until hot. Serve hot with ice-cream or allowable topping. Sufficient for 12 pancakes.

Layered Peach Filling

4 large ripe fresh peaches (golden-fleshed ones are best)
½ teaspoon ground cinnamon
2 tablespoons orange or pineapple juice
½ cup orange or pineapple juice
¾-1 cup stewed and puréed fresh apricots or homemade Apricot Jam (see recipe p. 92)
1 cup ground almonds

Peel the peaches by dipping them in boiling water, then slipping off the skins; cut them in half, remove stone and slice the flesh. Reserving six to eight of the best peach slices for decoration, place the remaining slices in a mixing bowl and fold through the cinnamon and the 2 tablespoons of juice.

To arrange layers, place a pancake in the centre of an oven-proof serving plate, spread 2-3 tablespoons of the peach mixture over the pancake and sprinkle with 1 tablespoon of the ½ cup of juice. Place the second pancake on top, spread with 2 table-spoons of apricot and sprinkle 2 tablespoons of ground almonds over the apricots; cover with another pancake. Repeat the alternate layers of peaches then apricots and almonds between pancakes, and finish with a pancake on top. Decorate with reserved peach slices, sprinkle with ground almonds and warm in a slow oven, 150°C (300°F), for 15-20 minutes. Serve warm or cold, cut into wedges like a cake and accompanied by ice-cream or allowable topping. Sufficient for 12 pancakes.

Banana Apricot Filling

4 mashed bananas
4 tablespoons puréed fresh apricots
1 tablespoon fresh mandarine or orange juice or 1 teaspoon lemon juice plus 3 teaspoons water
extra ½ cup juice

Mix together the above ingredients, except the extra juice. Fill the pancakes, roll them up and place, folded side down, in a greased ovenproof dish. Pour over the extra juice and bake in a moderate oven, 180°C (350°F), for 20-25 minutes or until hot. Sufficient for 6-8 pancakes.

Creamy Strawberry Filling

½ cup Goat's-milk Cottage Cheese (see recipe p. 87)
½ teaspoon vanilla essence
½ teaspoon finely grated lemon rind
¼ teaspoon ground cinnamon
½ cup chopped fresh strawberries, washed and hulled
fructose or honey to taste or 1 tablespoon sultanas puréed with the cottage cheese

Mix the cottage cheese with the other ingredients and spread the mixture over the warm pancakes. Serve pancakes in a layered gateau, rolled up or folded into triangles. Sufficient for 8 pancakes.

These are a few ideas for pancake desserts. Fresh fruit salad may also be used, or simply freshly stewed fruit in season spread over the pancakes, which are then folded into triangles and served with allowable topping. Possible toppings are: Goat's Milk Ice-cream, p. 174; Frozen Fruit Topping, p. 172; Creamed Goat's-milk Cottage Cheese, p. 87; Whipped Cream Substitute, p. 156.

Cold Desserts

In any of the uncooked desserts, Equal (see ''Sweeteners'', p. 20) may be used as an alternative sweetener.

Ambrosia

> 1 heaped tablespoon gelatine
> 1 cup hot water
> juice 3 large oranges
> juice 1 lemon
> 3 eggs, separated
> 1 tablespoon fructose or 2 tablespoons honey or ½ cup sultanas liquefied with the juice

To make this special vitamin- and protein-filled jelly dessert, first melt the gelatine in the hot water and allow to cool; add juice of oranges and lemon. In a large deep-sided serving dish, beat the egg yolks and fructose or honey till light and fluffy, then add the fruit juice and gelatine gradually, beating again. Add the stiffly beaten eggwhites, stirring carefully until the mixture is evenly blended. Chill until the jelly is set. Serves 6.

Banana Passionfruit Cream

    1 tablespoon gelatine
    4 tablespoons cold water
    1¼ cups banana
    2 teaspoons lemon juice
    1 tablespoon orange juice
    1 teaspoon grated orange rind
    ½ teaspoon grated lemon rind
    1 dessertspoon fructose or 1 tablespoon honey or 1 tablespoon
        sultanas liquefied with the juices plus 1 extra tablespoon water
    2 eggs, separated
    3-4 passionfruit

Soak the gelatine in the cold water. Mash the banana with the
juices and the rinds and stir in the fructose or honey and the
beaten egg yolks. Place mixture in a double boiler and heat
gently; then add the gelatine and heat until the mixture
thickens, stirring constantly. Remove from the heat to prevent
curdling and allow to cool. Fold in the stiffly beaten eggwhites
as soon as the mixture begins to firm and spoon into individual
dishes or place in a serving bowl; spoon passionfruit pulp over
the top. Allow to set in the refrigerator. This dessert may be
served with custard, ice-cream or other allowable topping.
Serves 4.

Cheesecakes

The following recipes are for those who can use goat's-milk
cottage cheese or tofu. See recipes on p. 87 for Goat's-milk
Cottage Cheese and on p. 88 for Tofu.

Cheesecake Crust

    2 slices allowable bread
    2 teaspoons melted margarine
    ¼ cup water

Toast and crumb the bread, then mix with the margarine and

water. Line a pie dish with the crumbs and bake at 200°C (400°F) for 12 minutes. Allow the crust to cool while preparing one of the following fillings.

Orange Cheesecake

3 dessertspoons gelatine
3 tablespoons water
¼ cup boiling water
250 g (8 oz) goat's-milk cottage cheese or *tofu*
sweetener to taste, e.g. ½ cup sultanas liquidised with the orange juice, or *Equal, honey* or *fructose* to taste
½ cup orange juice
1 teaspoon grated lemon rind
1 teaspoon grated orange rind
3 eggwhites

Soften the gelatine in the cold water then add the boiling water to dissolve it. Cream the cheese or tofu gradually, adding sweetener, orange juice and rinds; add gelatine mixture and beat again. Fold in the stiffly beaten eggwhites, pour onto crust and refrigerate until set. Serves 8.

Pineapple Lemon Cheesecake

500 g (1 lb) goat's-milk cottage cheese or *tofu*
½ cup sultanas blended in ½ cup fresh or *unsweetened pineapple juice*
½ teaspoon vanilla essence
juice of 2 lemons (or less if preferred)
rind of 1 lemon
1 tablespoon gelatine dissolved in ½ cup hot water
1 can unsweetened pineapple pieces or fresh ripe chopped pineapple
1 beaten eggwhite

Beat together the cottage cheese, sultana mixture, vanilla, lemon juice and rind, ½ cup of juice from tin and the gelatine

171

till the mixture is smooth. Fold in the pineapple pieces, cut into smaller chunks. Fold in the eggwhite, pour the mixture into a dish and top with pineapple pieces. Chill before serving. Serves 8-10.

Frozen Fruit Topping or Ice-cream

This is a very quick and versatile recipe. The Banana Topping version is always a catchcry from my children when they learn that I have not made a dessert for a meal. The frozen fruit toppings must be used immediately if a thick creamy topping is required, so whip it up in your food processor between main course and dessert. If it is not all used immediately, place any remainder in the freezer so it does not melt before it is time for second helpings. If left in the freezer for any length of time, the topping will freeze very hard so it will need to be part-thawed again before being used as a fruit-ice or gelato. A popular way to use up left-over fruit topping in my household is to spoon it, while still creamy, into icy-pole moulds and then freeze it hard for an after-school treat. The creamy topping may be used to top fresh fruit salad, Banana Sundaes (p. 175) or others of the desserts in this chapter. If made thick enough (using only ¼ cup milk to about 1½ cups frozen fruit), my children enjoy it plain, too, sometimes with the addition of chopped nuts.

To make the topping into an ice-cream mould, which is useful as a special dessert in place of commercial ice-cream, simply add to the prepared fruit topping 1 teaspoon of gelatine dissolved in ¼ cup of hot water (per 1½ cups frozen fruit or ½ cup milk used) and blend thoroughly. The addition of a ¼ cup coconut, if allowed, is beneficial but optional. Pour the mixture into a wetted mould and freeze until firm. Unmould the topping while still firm onto a serving plate by dipping the mould briefly in hot water. Allow the ice to thaw in the refrigerator for a couple of hours, or until it can be cut without difficulty. A decorative, layered dessert may be made by adding strawberry and banana to the mould, which makes a good two-layered mould.

The following topping recipes yield 2-3 cups.

Basic Fruit Topping

1½ cups frozen fruit, e.g. strawberries, bananas, pineapple
½-1 cup chilled goat's or soya milk or goat's yoghurt
(½ yoghurt, ½ water if preferred)

Place the frozen fruit in a food processor and process until well chopped. With motor running, gradually add the milk through the feed tube until the desired consistency is reached. Use as outlined above.

Banana Topping

3 medium frozen bananas
2 tablespoons coconut (optional)
½-1 cup goat's milk
½-1 teaspoon vanilla essence (optional)

To freeze the bananas, simply peel them, place in a plastic bag, seal and freeze. This is a good way to store bananas that are ripening more quickly than you can use them. Dice the frozen bananas into large chunks and proccess them in a food processor with the coconut until well chopped. Add the milk gradually until desired consistency is reached. Use as a topping over fruit salad or puddings, or serve plain with the addition of chopped walnuts or toasted almonds. It is excellent as an iced mould or in icy-poles, as the bananas produce a more creamy ice than do fruits with a higher water content, such as strawberries or pineapple.

Strawberry Topping 1

1 cup frozen strawberries
¼ cup coconut
¼-½ cup goat's milk

Place the strawberries and the coconut in a food processor and process until well chopped. Add the milk gradually, and continue blending until the desired consistency is reached.

Strawberry Topping 2

1 cup frozen strawberries
1 rounded teaspoon fructose or other sweetener
¼-½ cup goat's milk

Place the strawberries in a food processor with the fructose and process until well chopped. Gradually add the milk, continuing to blend, until the desired consistency is reached.

Fruit Salad Topping

3 medium frozen bananas
½ cup frozen strawberries
½ cup diced and frozen pineapple
2 tablespoons coconut
½-1 cup goat's milk
1 teaspoon vanilla essence

Place the fruit in a food processor and process until well chopped. Add the coconut, the milk and the vanilla and continue to blend until the desired consistency is reached.

Goat's or Soya Milk Ice-cream

500 ml (1 pt) goat's or soya milk
2 level teaspoons gelatine
2 level teaspoons arrowroot
2-4 teaspoons fructose or honey to taste or ¼ cup sultanas liquefied in some of the milk
1 teaspoon vanilla essence (increase if using soya milk, if preferred)
1 tablespoon margarine

Heat the milk; mix together the gelatine, arrowroot and fructose and add a little of the hot milk to the gelatine mixture. Stir well, then add to the remainder of the hot milk (with the honey if used), stirring constantly till the mixture thickens a little. Add the vanilla and margarine and stir until the margarine has melted and is well blended. Cool, then freeze until almost firm.

Beat with an electric beater until smooth then return the ice-cream to the freezer and freeze until just set but not too hard. Use the same day as it is made—it goes very hard if frozen overnight. Makes about ½ litre (1 pint) ice-cream.

Variations on this ice-cream could be:

• Chocolate or Carob Ice-cream—add 1 dessertspoon, or more to taste, of cocoa or carob powder when beating up the semi-frozen ice-cream.
• Strawberry—add, at the final beating, 1 cup of fresh puréed strawberries; check for sweetness as strawberries are not always very sweet.
• Apple Pie—add, at the final beating, ¾ cup of puréed stewed apple (unsweetened), a big pinch of ground cloves and ¼ teaspoon of cinnamon. Refreeze until the ice-cream is only just set.
• Apricot—add, at final beating, 1 cup of puréed apricots and 1 teaspoon of grated orange rind.
• Add, at final beating, ½ cup or more of additive-free fruit juice concentrate (see Sundaes below).

Sundaes

For a quick dessert, try any of these sundae suggestions:

• Banana Topping over fresh strawberries with a sprinkling of walnuts.
• Banana Split—slice a banana (per person) in half lengthways and place in individual dishes. Add scoops of vanilla-flavoured goat's milk ice-cream, pour over a little unsweetened apple and boysenberry fruit juice concentrate and sprinkle with chopped nuts, toasted if liked. (The fruit juice concentrate may be obtained from some health-food stores—it has no sugar or artificial additives.)

Or, to the sliced banana, add scoops of vanilla, strawberry and/or carob ice-cream and spoon over a little warmed Honey Caramel Sauce (it will become runny when warmed), see recipe on p. 46; top with toasted chopped nuts.

Or, in place of the fruit juice concentrate or the Honey

Caramel Sauce, use thin fruit purées, such as apricot or berry fruit and use toasted coconut in place of the chopped nuts.

• Scoops of vanilla goat's milk ice-cream with Chocolate-type Carob Sauce (see recipe on p. 47) poured over and chilled to give a hard chocolate-like coating (similar to the ice-creams available at cinemas); sprinkle with toasted chopped nuts or coconut.

Strawberry Passionfruit Parfait

1 egg
1 tablespoon fructose or honey or 2 tablespoons sultanas liquefied in the milk
1 tablespoon gelatine
1 cup boiling water
finely grated rind of 1 lemon
1 tablespoon lemon juice
1 cup goat's milk
2 teaspoons margarine
extra ¼ cup lemon juice to taste
1 cup sliced strawberries
pulp of 6 passionfruit

Beat the egg and fructose or honey together until light. Dissolve the gelatine in the boiling water and add the rind and tablespoon of lemon juice. Stir in the egg mixture with the goat's milk (and sultanas if used) and margarine. Stir till the margarine is melted and the ingredients are well blended; leave to almost set. Then whip the mixture until light, adding extra lemon juice to taste; fold in the strawberries and passionfruit and check the lemon-juice flavouring. Fold into individual parfait glasses or sweet dishes and chill until set. Serve chilled, decorated with a spoonful of creamed goat's cottage cheese, if desired, and extra whole strawberries. The parfait may be used to fill Coconut Macaroon Pavlova, p. 188 (in which case it serves 8). Serves 6.

Tropical Yoghurt Mould

2 tablespoons gelatine
½ cup hot water
2 cups prepared Boiled Custard (see recipe p. 46)
400 g (12 oz) unsweetened goat's yoghurt
1 cup finely chopped fresh fruit salad (ripe apple, pear, apricots, orange and passionfruit, but not fresh pineapple in a gelatine pudding—see p. 178)
½ cup orange juice

Sprinkle the gelatine over the water, stir until dissolved and blend into the custard. Stir in the remaining ingredients and check the flavour, adding more orange juice if a more fruity flavour is preferred. Pour into a six-cup ring mould and chill until firm. Turn out of mould and serve with the middle filled with fresh pineapple and decorated with sliced Kiwi fruit. Serves 6-8.

Yoghurt Filling

1 tablespoon gelatine
3 tablespoons water
1 dessertspoon fructose or 1 tablespoon honey or 2 tablespoons sultanas liquefied in the yoghurt
½ teaspoon vanilla essence
fresh fruit for flavour, e.g. pulp of 2 or more passionfruit
1 cup plain unsweetened goat's yoghurt
1 eggwhite

Soak the gelatine in the water, then heat, stirring until the gelatine is dissolved. Add the honey (if used) and cool slightly. Add the fructose, vanilla and fruit to the yoghurt (and sultanas if used), then stir in the gelatine mixture. Fold in the stiffly beaten eggwhite and chill until nearly set.

Fresh Fruit Salad

An allergy to oranges does not prevent you from making a fresh fruit salad; simply place a mixture of ¼ teaspoon Vitamin C powder per half a cup of water in a salad bowl, cut up any fruit as desired and add to the bowl, coating the pieces well with the Vitamin C mixture which will prevent any discolouration. Adjust the liquid mixture to suit the quantity of salad you are making. You may even find that you prefer fruit salad without oranges, as our family does.

Fruit Tarts

Fruit tarts or flans can be served all year round using fruits in season, and may be served either hot or cold with the tart case precooked or cooked along with the fruit after the uncooked case has been filled.

If pre-cooking the tart case (known as "blind" baking), roll out the pastry to fit the flan tin, then place a piece of greaseproof paper over the base of the tart case and sprinkle a tablespoon of uncooked rice or lentils on top—this prevents the base rising up during baking and spoiling the case shape. If there is any doubt about the soundness of the case once cooked, an eggwhite spread around the case to coat it while still hot will help to seal it. A cooked case may be filled with hot stewed fruit or cold fruit pieces either sliced or simply washed, halved and stoned (if applicable) and then packed decoratively into the case. A small amount of fruit juice (with a ¼ teaspoon of vitamin C powder added if the fruit has a tendency to brown) drizzled over the fruit completes the tart.

Cold fruit tarts may be made even more special by glazing with jellied fruit juice. Reserve one cupful or so of the juice from the stewed fruit, or liquefy or purée extra fruit, adding water to make a cupful if the purée is very thick. Heat the juice, stir in ½-1 teaspoon of gelatine (depending on firmness required) and stir till dissolved; add sweetener if desired. Spoon the warm glaze over the fruit in the flan to fill the spaces between fruit and to coat the fruit segments evenly, then chill until the glaze is firm. Apricot halves are particularly good in a glazed tart; if you live in the country, try glazing your next blackberry tart and serving it cold.

An old-time favourite for hot tarts is the combination of blackberry and apple—perhaps use some blackberries frozen during late summer and combined in winter with the new season's apples. Another delicious winter tart is the following, to which I was introduced in England under very snowy conditions.

Pear and Apricot Flan

100 g (3 oz) apricots (frozen, unsweetened tinned or dried if tolerated)
lemon juice to coat pears or water with ¼ teaspoon vitamin C powder
2-3 firm ripe pears
pastry to fit 20 cm (8 in) flan tin
½ teaspoon ground cinnamon

Prepare the apricots *either* by thawing frozen apricots by simmering them gently in a pan, reserving the juices formed and halving the apricots; *or* halve tinned apricots if necessary and reserve the juice; *or* soak dried apricots in cold water overnight or place in a pan with 2 cups of water, bring to boil, remove from heat and leave for 30 minutes; then halve the apricots and reserve the liquid.

Place the lemon juice or vitamin C mixture in a saucer; peel, core and quarter the pears and coat them in the juice to prevent browning. Place a layer of half the pears on the base of the pastry-lined flan case, add half the apricots and sprinkle with cinnamon. Cover with remaining pears and apricots and sprinkle with remaining cinnamon. Drizzle a little of the reserved juice over, to just moisten the fruit, and bake the flan in a moderately hot oven, 190°C (375°F), for 40-45 minutes or until the pastry is cooked and the fruit softened. Serve warm or cold with custard, goat's ice-cream or other allowable topping. Serves 6-8.

14
SPECIAL
OCCASIONS

In the following recipes, use whichever flour suits your needs best—see Chapters 7 and 11 for guidelines. Also, those who are able may wish to add a little sherry or brandy to the Christmas recipes.

Traditional Christmas Cake

> 125 g (4 oz) natural dried apricots
> 125 g (4 oz) fresh stoned cherries
> 300 g (10 oz) sultanas
> 200 g (6 oz) currants
> grated rind 1 orange
> grated rind 1 lemon
> ¾ cup grated carrot
> 125 g (4 oz) margarine
> 1 cup water
> 1½ teaspoons mixed spice
> 2¼ cups flour, e.g. 1 cup brown-rice flour and 1¼ cups rice bran or 1 cup soya flour and 1¼ cups brown-rice flour
> 1 teaspoon bicarbonate of soda
> 2 teaspoons cream of tartar
> ¾ cup fresh or unsweetened tinned orange or pineapple juice or water
> halved blanched almonds (for decoration)

Prepare a 20 cm (8 in) round cake tin by lining it with foil and then with greased greaseproof paper. Preheat the oven to 180°C (350°F).

Chop the dried apricots, halve the stoned cherries and rinse the dried fruit thoroughly. Boil together gently for five minutes the dried fruit, cherries, rinds, carrot, margarine, water and mixed spice; then allow the mixture to cool. Sift the flour, soda and cream of tartar together and add to the fruit mixture alternatively with the juice. Spoon the mixture into the prepared tin and arrange the almonds decoratively on the top. Place in a preheated oven, turned down to 160°C (325°F), and place a sheet of greaseproof paper over the top of the cake. Bake for about two hours, or until an inserted skewer comes out clean, and remove the cover to brown the almonds during the final 30 minutes or so. Cool thoroughly before cutting. If made with wholly rice flour, this cake does not freeze well as it becomes crumbly on thawing. Because of the fresh fruit in the cake it should be eaten within a week of baking and should also be stored in the refrigerator.

Light Christmas Cake

  100 g (3 oz) pitted and chopped prunes
  100 g (3 oz) chopped dried apricots
  100 g (3 oz) sultanas
  100 g (3 oz) halved fresh pitted cherries
  1 medium grated carrot
  ¾ cup water
  125 g (4 oz) margarine
  2½ cups flour, e.g. 1 cup each of rice bran and brown-rice flour
      and ½ cup arrowroot or 1¼ cups each of soya flour and
      brown-rice flour
  1¼ teaspoons bicarbonate of soda
  2½ teaspoons cream of tartar
  1 teaspoon mixed spice
  extra ¾-1 cup water
  75 g (2½ oz) sliced brazil nuts

Line a 20 cm (8 in) tin with foil on the bottom and sides and then with greased greaseproof paper. Preheat the oven to 180°C (350°F).

Rinse the dried fruit thoroughly and place the dried fruit, cherries, carrot, ¾ cup water and margarine in a saucepan and boil together gently for five minutes. Allow the mixture to cool. Sift the flour with the soda, cream of tartar and mixed spice and add to the fruit mixture alternately with the extra water; fold in the brazil nuts. Turn mixture into the prepared tin and bake, covered with greaseproof paper, for two hours or until an inserted skewer comes out clean. Wrap and cool thoroughly before cutting. Do not freeze the cake if made from wholly rice flour, as it becomes crumbly on thawing. Refrigerate if keeping but use the cake within one week.

Pumpkin Christmas Cake

1 cup sultanas
1 cup currants
½ cup chopped raisins
2 cups water
1½ cups cold mashed butternut pumpkin
2 teaspoons grated lemon rind
3 tablespoons oil
1½ cups soya flour
1½ cups brown-rice flour
1½ teaspoons bicarbonate of soda
3 teaspoons cream of tartar
1 teaspoon mixed spice
1 teaspoon nutmeg
1 teaspoon cinnamon

Rinse the dried fruit well in hot water and combine the fruit and water in a large saucepan. Bring to the boil, remove from the heat and stir in the pumpkin, lemon rind and oil; allow to cool and then stir in the sifted dry ingredients. Spread the mixture into a greased and lined 20 cm (8 in) deep round cake tin and bake in a moderately slow oven, 160°C (325°F), for

1½-2 hours, or until the cake is cooked when tested. Cover and cool overnight in the tin. Store the cake in the refrigerator but do not keep for more than one week. The pumpkin used in the cake is purely mashed pumpkin—do not mash it with milk, margarine, etcetera, as this recipe is egg-, milk- and sweetener-free.

Shortbread

Two recipes are given here for those with grain allergies who crave shortbread. The wholly rice flour recipe is more manageable if kept in, and used straight from, the freezer or at least the refrigerator. The soya-rice recipe may be made in the traditional shortbread shape or else rolled thinly and made into little shortbread biscuits with fancy biscuit cutters, such as star shapes for Christmas. These are very popular with children.

Shortbread 1

> 200 g (7 oz) margarine
> 1 tablespoon fructose
> ½ cup arrowroot
> 1½ cups rice bran
> ½ cup brown-rice flour
> ½ level teaspoon bicarbonate of soda
> 1 level teaspoon cream of tartar

Cream the margarine and fructose; sift the flours, soda and cream of tartar and work into the creamed mixture. Spread the mixture into two 18 cm (7 in) sandwich tins and bake for 25 minutes at 180°C (350°F). Allow to cool and store chilled.

Shortbread 2

²/₃ cup soya flour
½ cup brown-rice flour
1 tablespoon fructose
1 tablespoon arrowroot
125 g (4 oz) margarine
1 egg yolk

Mix the flours, fructose and arrowroot evenly, then rub in the margarine till blended. Add the egg yolk and mix to a dough, *or* place all ingredients in a food processor and process until a ball forms. Press the dough into one 20 cm (8 in) sandwich tin for the traditional shortbread shape. Bake for 25 minutes at 180°C (350°F) until lightly browned. Alternatively roll the dough out thinly using a sheet of greaseproof paper or waxed lunch wrap between the rolling pin and dough for easier rolling. Cut the dough into fancy shapes and bake on lightly greased trays for 10-15 minutes at 180°C (350°F) or until lightly browned. Cool and store in an airtight container.

Santa's Buttons

1 quantity Freezer Slice mixture (p. 152)
extra 1¼ cup coconut
coconut for rolling
cherries, blanched almonds or dried apricots (for decoration)

Add the extra coconut to the mixture and form teaspoonfuls of the mixture into small balls using your wet fingers. Roll the balls in coconut and top each one with halved and pitted fresh cherries, halved blanched almonds or pieces of dried apricot, soaked to soften them. Bake in a 160°C (325°F) oven for 20 minutes or until just turning golden.

These biscuits are named after biscuits that my children used to leave for Santa on Christmas Eve. They were delighted when I adapted another recipe to make the following version. These biscuits are, of course, generally useful at Christmas time or as a special fruit biscuit at other times. Makes 24.

White Christmas

⅓ cup pitted and halved fresh cherries
1 quantity Copha Slice (p. 152)

Drain well any surplus juice from the cherries to prevent staining the mixture too much. Fold the cherries through the slice mixture evenly and quickly. Spread the mixture in a 20 cm (8 in) square slice tin and refrigerate until firm. Cut into squares.

Traditional Christmas Pudding

300 g (9 oz) raisins
300 g (9 oz) sultanas
125 g (4 oz) currants
100 g (3 oz) pitted and chopped prunes
rind 1 lemon and 1 orange
50 g (1½ oz) coarsely chopped blanched almonds
1 medium grated carrot
250 g (8 oz) soft breadcrumbs from any tolerated bread (reduce to 125 g (4 oz) if soft wheat bread is used as it is lighter than non-wheat bread)
⅓ cup brown-rice flour } or other tolerated flours
½ cup rice bran
1 teaspoon nutmeg
1 teaspoon mixed spice
⅔ cup goat's or soya milk
1 cup orange juice

This recipe is egg-, fat- and sweetener-free; it may also be milk-free.

Rinse the dried fruit well and mix the fruit, rinds, almonds, carrot and breadcrumbs together in a bowl. Sift the flour and bran, nutmeg and mixed spice and add to the fruit alternately with the milk and orange juice. Turn into a greased basin (or basins), cover with greaseproof paper and aluminium foil and secure with string. Steam the pudding in a saucepan, with the water coming halfway up the sides of the basins, for four hours. Cool and refrigerate if the pudding is to be used within a few days; if not, freeze it. Before using, steam again for one hour, turn out and serve the pudding hot with custard and ice-cream or other topping. The recipe makes one large pudding, or one medium and one small pudding.

Christmas Neapolitan Ice

1½ cups finely chopped mixed fruit, e.g. ½ cup sultanas, ½ cup fresh cherries, ¼ cup prunes, ¼ cup dried apricots
¾ cup fresh or unsweetened tinned fruit juice (orange, pineapple, apricot)
750 ml-1 litre (1½-2 pt) goat's milk ice-cream
about 1 cup fresh strawberries
1 tablespoon fructose or honey
3 dessertspoons carob powder or cocoa to taste
3 tablespoons water
3 egg yolks
1¼ cups goat's-milk cottage cheese
½ teaspoon vanilla essence (or to taste)
¼ cup toasted almonds or other chopped nuts (optional)

Marinate the chopped mixed fruit in the fruit juice while preparing the ice-cream layers. Prepare the ice-cream up to the final beating stage, then divide into three and work quickly. Leave one portion plain; flavour one portion with about 1 cup of fresh puréed strawberries (amount depends on strength of flavour) and add ½ teaspoon or so of fructose or a teaspoon of honey if the strawberries are tart. Flavour the third portion with carob or cocoa to taste. Replace each portion in the freezer once it is well beaten and smooth so it remains (or becomes) firm.

Line a large freeze-proof bowl of about 20 cm (8 in) diameter (or a mould) with layers of ice-cream in the following way: spoon the carob layer into the bottom of the bowl. Place a small bowl of 14 cm (5½ in) diameter on the carob layer to form a cavity for the fruit mixture. Spoon half the vanilla portion around the sides of the carob layer, then spoon the strawberry ice-cream onto the vanilla layer once it is just firm enough to prevent the layers mixing. Reserving enough vanilla ice-cream to cover the top of the pudding, use any remainder on top of the strawberry to bring the ice-cream level up to the top of the small bowl. If the small bowl tends to rise up too much, place a screw-top jar three-quarters filled with water inside the bowl to weight it down. Freeze the ice-cream until firm enough to hold its shape when the bowl is removed. To remove the small bowl, fill it with warm water for a minute or so to loosen it, tip the water out and then slip the bowl out. Fill the remaining cavity with the prepared fruit and egg mixture and cover with the remaining vanilla ice-cream. Freeze the pudding until firm but still soft enough to be cut.

To prepare the fruit and egg filling, make a syrup from the fructose or honey and water and let it cool. Beat the yolks until light and creamy, place them in a saucepan and add the syrup gradually over a low heat, stirring constantly until the mixture thickens. Remove pan from the heat and cool the mixture in a basin of cold water, whisking until it is smooth and cooled. Beat the goat's cottage cheese until smooth, adding a little extra goat's milk to make a whipped-cream consistency, and flavour with vanilla essence. Add with the marinated fruit to the egg mixture, mixing well and add the nuts (if used). Spoon the mixture into the cavity in the ice-cream mould.

If prepared in advance and frozen solid, this pudding will take up to six to seven hours to thaw in the bottom of the refrigerator. Unmould it while still solid onto a serving plate (by dipping the bowl briefly in hot water) *before* thawing—a soft ice-cream is difficult to unmould successfully. For a spectacular Christmas bombe, this dessert could be coated with Coconut Macaroon meringue (see recipe p. 116), browned very lightly in the oven and then flamed if alcohol is tolerated. A delicious alternative to the usual hot Christmas pudding or as a treat for Christmas tea for a large gathering. Make the ice at least a full day in advance as the layers ideally need time to firm up between additions. Serves 12-14.

Coconut Macaroon Pavlova

arrowroot
1 quantity Coconut Macaroon mixture (p. 116)

Grease a pavlova plate, dust with arrowroot and spread the prepared Coconut Macaroon mixture over the pavlova plate, heaping the mixture up at the sides to form a case. Bake in a slow oven, 150°C (300°F), for 30-45 minutes or until set. Allow the pavlova to cool; it may be made in advance and frozen. Serves 6.

Suitable fillings for the pavlova are as follows:

• Strawberry Passionfruit Parfait—see recipe on p. 176. Spoon the prepared mixture into a macaroon case after the strawberries and passionfruit have been folded in. Chill till the filling has set and decorate with extra whole strawberries and banana slices dipped in lemon juice.
• Frozen Fruit Ice-cream—see recipe on p. 172. Prepare a thick mixture and work quickly to fill the case. Freeze the Macaroon Pavlova until the filling is set to an iced-mousse consistency and serve decorated with appropriate extra fresh fruit.

Coconut Macaroon Cigars

1 quantity Coconut Macaroon mixture (p. 116)
special diet chocolate (sugar- and milk-free, obtainable at health-
  food stores and confectionery (sweets) shops)
1 teaspoon margarine

Spoon the prepared mixture into finger-length cigar shapes on the prepared oven trays. Bake for 30 minutes or until set at 150°C (300°F) and cool on a wire rack.

Melt the chocolate with a teaspoon or so of margarine, stirring well, and dip one end of the "cigars" into the chocolate. (The chocolate may also be spooned over rather than the biscuit dipped in.) Place on waxed paper to dry and set. Makes about 8 "cigars".

The chocolate may be spooned over as a topping for macaroon mounds, if this shape is preferred. These are useful served as after-dinner biscuits.

Allergy-free "Rum" Balls

½ cup water
1 dessertspoon (or less) fructose or 1 dessertspoon honey or 1 tablespoon sultanas liquefied in the water (optional)
½ cup margarine
½ cup sultanas
½ cup coconut
¼ cup cocoa or carob powder
2 cups (or more) rolled oats or other rolled grain
extra coconut

Heat the water, sweetener (if used) and margarine in a medium-sized saucepan over a medium heat until the margarine is melted and the sweetener dissolved; allow to cool. Add sultanas, coconut, cocoa or carob and oats and mix to a stiff consistency; then form into balls and roll them in the coconut.

If rolled rice is used, add the rice to the liquid in the saucepan. Add an extra ¾ cup water and stir while heating gently, until all the liquid has been absorbed. Then add the remaining ingredients.

The mixture may need to be refrigerated until it is firm enough to form into balls if it is too soft and warm. Store balls in the refrigerator. Makes about 36 balls.

A variation on the above recipe is:

Apricot or Peach Balls

Omit the ½ cup of sultanas and use well-drained, stewed peaches or apricots, reserving the liquid to be used in place of the ½ cup of water. Chill the mixture before forming into balls. Make some of each of the "rum" and apricot balls—they are decorative served together and contrast well in taste.

Cherry Duckling

1 large duck (2½ kg (5 lb) dressed weight)
250 g (8 oz) goat's-milk cottage cheese
3 heaped tablespoons muesli (see recipe p. 67)
350 g (11 oz) fresh black or white cherries
brown-rice flour for dusting
200 ml (⅓ pt) water
2 teaspoons fructose or honey to taste (optional)
1 dessertspoon or so arrowroot

Thaw the duck thoroughly if it is frozen. Preheat the oven to 190°C (375°F).

To prepare the stuffing, combine the cheese, muesli and 125 g (4 oz) of the pitted and halved cherries. Place the stuffing in neck end of the duck, prick skin on breast and leg, place in a roasting tin or on a rack and cover with foil. Cook for one hour at 190°C (350°F); then remove foil, prick again and dust with brown-rice flour to crispen and bake for an extra 30 minutes or until the duck is tender.

Pit the remaining cherries and simmer gently in water and sweetener (if used) for three minutes only (the rich colour pales if cherries are cooked longer). Remove the duck to a serving dish and keep warm while making the cherry sauce—drain the fat from the roasting dish, add the juice from the simmered cherries and bring to the boil and thicken slightly with a little arrowroot blended to a paste in a little cold water. Add the cherries to the sauce and spoon over the duck or serve separately.

This special dish, with its unusual stuffing and sauce, is especially suitable for an Australian Christmas, as fresh cherries are in season then. Serves 4-6.

Turkey-filled Pancakes

2 cups cooked diced turkey
1 cup turkey stuffing
1 cup turkey gravy or stock
1 egg
1 tablespoon chopped parsley
Cherry "Cranberry" Sauce (see recipe p. 47)

Mix the turkey, stuffing and gravy together well in a bowl.
Add the beaten egg and mix well, and then add the parsley and
mix through. Place filling on pancakes, roll up and bake, packing
them side by side in a greased baking dish, in a moderate oven,
180°C (350°F), for 20 minutes or until hot. Serve accompanied
by the fresh Cherry Sauce. These are a delicious way to use up
the last of the Christmas turkey. The recipe makes sufficient for
10-12 pancakes.

Birthday Party Fare

Here are some suggestions for what may be served at a
children's birthday party when either your children or the
guests have food allergies, or you simply wish to avoid the
artificial additives of commercial "party food".

Choose from these recipes depending on the ages of the
children:

- Party Mince Pies—made in patty-tin size (see recipe p. 197).
- Sausage Rolls—homemade and pastry- or pancake-encased,
then sliced into segments.
- Sausages—made small like cocktail frankfurters or larger ones
cut in chunks and served on toothpicks for dipping into a sauce
(see recipes pp. 59-61).
- Sweetcorn—cut in rings, freshly cooked and served hot.
- Home-cooked popcorn—cooked in allowable oil, unsalted
and tossed in a little honey if tolerated. Serve warm—the
cooking instructions are usually on the packet.
- Homemade Tomato Sauce (see recipes pp. 33 and 45).

- Patty Cakes—made with tolerated flour (see recipe p. 141).
- Carob or Cocoa Crackles—made from allowable grains and without sugar (see recipe p. 115).
- "Rum" and/or Apricot Balls (see recipe p. 189).
- Hedgehog Slice (see recipe p. 153).
- Copha Slice (see recipe p. 152). This is good if any allergy to cocoa and carob exists.
- Bowls of special fresh fruits—presented decoratively, in the place of commercial lollies, such as whole strawberries, washed and hulled; fresh cherries if in season; hunks of watermelon; pineapple chunks or balls of rockmelon (cantaloupe). Have toothpicks available for ease of serving.
- Waffles—made from tolerated flour (see p. 93); serve them warm. They may be made in advance, frozen, then reheated when needed. Very popular with eight-year-olds and over, as they are a little more "grown-up".
- Any of the recipes from the confectionery chapter (pp. 201-205).
- Fresh Fruit Jellies (see recipe p. 196).
- Goat's Milk Ice-cream—flavoured or vanilla (see recipe p. 174).
- Birthday Cake—made from tolerated flour (see recipes pp. 193-195).
- Ice-cream Birthday Cake (see recipe p. 195).
- Fresh fruit juices made "effervescent" by the addition of mineral or soda water (see Chapter 1, p. 24).
- Fruit Punch (see recipe p. 25).

Commercially available products are a time-saver, if tolerated. Choose from the following:

- Unsalted additive-free corn chips—from health-food stores.
- Sugar- and artificial-additive-free tomato sauce—from health-food stores and some supermarkets.
- Sugar- and artificial-additive-free confectionery—such as carob-coated nuts and a few of the "health bars". Read the labels well as most carob confections contain powdered cow's milk.
- Unsalted peanuts and nuts.

• Sugar- and additive-free fruit juice concentrates—from health-food stores.
• Sugar-, colouring- and flavouring-free fruit juices—some are preservative-free also (apple and orange, for example), but read the labels carefully. Available from supermarkets and health-food stores.

As important, if not more important, than what the food is made of, is presentation. Children often do not notice ingredients—at least until later when they are happily without their usual after-party stomach upset, rash or upper respiratory allergy reaction. But children will be excited about presentation details—here are a few suggestions:

• "Rum" and Apricot Balls—secured with toothpicks to an orange in a dish.
• Patty Cakes—made in multicoloured paper cases instead of white cases.
• Carob Crackles—made in tiny petit four flowered or coloured paper cases.
• Decorative jelly moulds—a sound investment for parties; they come in rabbit, car, heart shapes, etcetera.
• Decorative party plates, serviettes and hats are also a must to set the scene at the party table.

Birthday Cakes

Basic Butter Cake

125 g (4 oz) softened margarine
1 tablespoon fructose or 2 tablespoons honey
1 teaspoon vanilla essence
2 eggs
1½ cups flour, e.g. ¾ cup soya flour and ¾ cup brown-rice
  flour
¾ teaspoon bicarbonate of soda
1½ teaspoons cream of tartar
½ cup goat's or soya milk or water

Cream the margarine and fructose or honey until light and fluffy. Beat in the vanilla, and add the eggs, one at a time, and beat well. Sift the flours with the soda and cream of tartar and lightly stir in alternately with the liquid. Spread the mixture into a 20 cm (8 in) round or other chosen tin and bake in a moderately hot oven, 190°C (375°F), until the cake is golden and the centre springs back when touched—approximately 30-45 minutes, depending on size and shape of tin used.

For shape ideas consult the *Australian Women's Weekly: Children's Birthday Cake Book* (Australian Consolidated Press), available from newsagents and book stores. There are numerous ideas in this book for decorations using things other than lollies. You may be able to incorporate on the cake one trinket for each guest which can be taken home after the party as a memento. Look for packets of toys tiny enought to fit on a cake when party-time approaches. Ribbon and lace can add the finishing touch to a cake instead of hundred's and thousand's. Fresh-fruit pieces may also be used for decoration, such as strawberries and sliced Kiwi fruit for a colour contrast—these are popular with the older primary-school child. For fillings and icings or toppings, consult Chapter 12.

Soya-oat Birthday Cake

375 g (12 oz) margarine
rind 1 orange
6 eggs
1 cup oat flour
1 cup brown-rice flour
2½ cups soya flour
2½ teaspoons cream of tartar
1¼ teaspoons bicarbonate of soda
1 mashed banana
juice 2 oranges
1 cup goat's or soya milk

Cream the margarine and rind together, and then beat in the eggs, one at a time. Sift the flours with the cream of tartar and soda. Add the banana and liquid alternately with the flour to the egg mixture, stirring lightly. Spread the mixture into three 20 cm (8 in) round tins and bake in a moderately hot oven, 190°C (375°F), until golden and the centre springs back when touched—about 30-45 minutes depending on the tins used.

The recipe makes a cake firm enough for elaborate constructions (even an upright "Fluffy Duck", coated in Coconut Macaroon, and transported from home to a nearby park!). The recipe makes three times the amount of the Basic Butter Cake recipe (p. 193), and is sweetener-free.

Soya-rice Birthday Cake

250 g (8 oz) margarine
2 teaspoons vanilla essence
4 eggs
1 cup brown-rice flour
1 cup rice bran
½ cup soya flour
½ cup arrowroot
1½ teaspoons bicarbonate of soda
3 teaspoons cream of tartar
½ cup pineapple juice
2 tablespoons sultanas liquefied in the juice (optional)

Cream the margarine until light and fluffy. Beat in the vanilla, and add the eggs, one at a time, and beat well. Sift the flours with the soda and cream of tartar and lightly stir in alternately with the liquid. Makes sufficient for a 20 cm (8 in) round and a 25 by 7.5 cm (10 by 3 in) log tin. Bake in a moderately hot oven, 190°C (375°F), until the cake is golden and the centre springs back when touched—approximately 30-45 minutes.

Neapolitan Ice-cream Cake

Since goat's milk ice-cream tends to be firmer than commercial ice-cream, it is ideal for an ice-cream cake which has to be able to stand at room temperature for a short while.

Simply make up the quantity of ice-cream required and divide the mixture, once it is nearly frozen, into three. Whip up the vanilla portion and return it to the freezer; add carob or cocoa to the second, whipping it until smooth and placing it also in the freezer; meanwhile, add the puréed strawberries and possibly sweetener to the third portion and whip it until smooth. Spoon ice-cream in layers into the chosen bowl, oblong dish or whatever you find suitable and freeze overnight or until firm. Thaw the ice-cream sufficiently in the bottom of the refrigerator before the party so that it can be cut. Trim into desired shape while still fairly firm and decorate as required. The ice-cream can be moulded with commercial moulds, but always unmould it while still frozen.

Fresh Fruit Jelly

fresh fruit
juice or *water to cover fruit*
1 tablespoon gelatine per 500 ml (1 pt) juice or *juice and fruit*

Place the fresh fruit in a saucepan, add liquid to just cover. Simmer gently for three to five minutes, add gelatine and stir until it is dissolved; also add sweetener if necessary. Pour into a wetted decorative or nursery mould, and chill until firm.

Cherries and blackberries make good red jellies—simmer cherries only briefly lest the colour changes to brown. Apricots, puréed or juiced, make tasty orange jellies. Granny Smith apple juice (with added vitamin C powder) gives a light-green jelly. Tinned unsweetened pineapple juice gives a yellow jelly. The colours may be combined, for example, strawberries or cherries jelled inside apricot or pineapple jelly. Construct two-tone jellies in the usual way.

Patty Cakes

See recipe on p. 141. Patty cakes may be decorated in a variety of ways: see Chapter 12. Favourites are Carob Icing sprinkled with coconut or whole chopped nuts; Goat's Cheese Mock Cream with a slice of strawberry, banana and some passionfruit pulp. Make some into "butterfly" cakes, too, perhaps filled with Banana Apricot Filling or Goat's Cheese Mock Cream.

Party Pies

> 250 g (8 oz) minced beef
> 1 small finely chopped onion
> 1 stick finely chopped celery
> 1 medium finely grated carrot
> water or stock
> black pepper to taste
> ¼ teaspoon ground oregano
> arrowroot for thickening
> 1 quantity meat pie pastry (see p. 105)
> a little beaten egg or milk or water to glaze

Sauté the beef gently in its own fat till brown, and pour off the excess fat. Add onion and celery and cook for five minutes. Add carrot, water or stock to cover, and seasoning, and cover and simmer for 30 minutes. Chill the meat mixture, skim off the fat and reheat. Mix the arrowroot with a little cold water to a paste, add to the hot meat and stir till thickened—the mixture needs to be fairly thick so it will not run out when the pies are eaten.

Roll out the pastry and cut into rounds to fit patty tins. Fill with the cooled meat mixture, cover with pastry and crimp the edges. Brush with beaten egg, milk or water and bake in a hot oven, 200°C (400°F), for 30 minutes or until pastry is cooked and golden. Makes about 1½ dozen.

Hot-cross Buns

Once you have made your own hot-cross buns—either yeast-risen or the soda-risen versions given here—I guarantee you will never willingly go back to the white-flour commercial ones. They freeze well so make them in advance and make a few extra buns, perhaps without the cross, for use a few weeks later. They are delicious served hot for a late-night casual supper, and are especially easy if you possess a microwave oven.

The ingredients for the different flour combinations are given first, then the method, which is common to all. All the recipes are yeast-free; they may be made milk-free and they contain no added sweetener beyond the dried fruit and the optional glaze. The following recipes each yield about 30 buns.

Wholewheat Hot-cross Buns

1 kg (2 lb) wholewheat flour
2 teaspoons bicarbonate of soda
4 teaspoons cream of tartar
3½ teaspoons mixed spice
2 teaspoons cinnamon
2 cups sultanas and/or currants (optional)
juice ½ lemon
3½-4 cups goat's or soya milk or water
1 cup water

Buckwheat, Rice and Potato Hot-cross Buns

200 g (6 oz) buckwheat flour
125 g (4 oz) brown-rice flour
125 g (4 oz) potato flour
1 teaspoon cinnamon
2 teaspoons mixed spice
1½ teaspoons bicarbonate of soda
3 teaspoons cream of tartar
1 cup sultanas and/or currants
1½-2 cups goat's or soya milk or water
1 tablespoon lemon juice

Soya-oat Hot-cross Buns

2¼ cups (12 oz) ground oats or oat flour
½ cup (4 oz) brown-rice flour
2 cups (12 oz) soya flour
1 cup (4 oz) rolled oats
2 teaspoons bicarbonate of soda
4 teaspoons cream of tartar
3½ teaspoons mixed spice
2 teaspoons cinnamon
2 cups sultanas and/or currants
juice ½ lemon
3½-4 cups goat's or soya milk or water
1 cup water

Soya-rice Hot-cross Buns

Omit the first four ingredients in the Soya-oat recipe and substitute:

2½ cups (16 oz) soya
  flour
1½ cups (8 oz) brown-   or
  rice flour
2 cups (8 oz) rice bran

2½ cups (16 oz) soya
  flour
3½ cups (16 oz) brown-
  rice flour

Remaining ingredients as in previous recipe.

Sift the flour (except rolled oats if used), spices, soda and cream of tartar and add the lemon juice to the milk or water. Place the sifted flour in a large mixing bowl, add the dried fruit and rolled oats (if used), make a well in the centre of the flour and add the liquid, mixing thoroughly. Spoon heaped tablespoonfuls of the mixture close together in greased lamington trays or cake tins with sides. Bake in a hot oven, 200°C (400°F), for about 45 minutes or until cooked through. Glaze the buns while still hot.

The crosses may be either piped on using Dairy-free Mock Cream (p. 155) or White Drizzle (p. 155); they are added to the cooked, glazed and cooled buns. Alternatively, use baked-on crosses, added before baking. Make a mixture of 4 tablespoons of brown-rice flour and 2 tablespoons of cold water (per 500 g (1 lb) of flour in bun recipe) and beat until smooth. Fill into a greaseproof paper funnel or biscuit forcing bag and pipe crosses over the buns.

Glaze:
  For each 12-16 buns allow:
  ¼ teaspoon gelatine
  2 tablespoons hot water
  1 teaspoon fructose or *2 teaspoons honey* or *to taste*

Combine the gelatine and water in a saucepan and heat over a low heat, stirring until gelatine is dissolved. Add sweetener and stir until dissolved or well blended. Brush the glaze over the buns while buns are still hot.

Easter Eggs

Make your own cocoa-, sugar- and milk-free Easter eggs, novelty shapes for children and shell or geometrical ones for adults (unless they would like the novelty ones too!). Use the coating mixture given in the Carob-coated Nuts 'n' Raisins recipe (p. 203). There are many plastic moulds in various shapes and sizes now readily available from department stores and specialty shops. These make solid confectionery. The above recipe is not suitable for coating the sides of a hollow Easter egg; for this purpose milk powder is necessary to thicken the mixture sufficiently. However, small solid Easter eggs can be made in two halves using the appropriate mould. Wrap the two halves together in some coloured foil for a commercial Easter-egg effect, so loved by children. My children were particularly delighted with the solid Easter ''bunnies'', and several different sizes of rabbit moulds are available, from tiny to jelly-mould size.

Novelty shapes can be used to cater for children on any special occasion, to decorate cakes or to serve after dinner with coffee even for non-allergic guests.

Store such confectionery in the refrigerator or in the freezer.

15
CONFECTIONERY

Sunflower-peanut (Soya Bean) Balls

½ cup peanut butter (sugar-free commercial kind or homemade,
  see recipe p. 90) or soya-bean butter (see recipe p. 89)
⅔ cup finely ground sunflower seeds
¼ cup finely chopped raisins
¼ cup finely chopped dates or other dried fruit
¼ cup goat's or soya milk powder
carob powder, cocoa or coconut for coating

Cream together the butter, sunflower seeds and dried fruit until
blended. Mix in the milk powder, using your fingers to knead,
and adjust the consistency with either some liquid milk or some
more powdered milk. Roll the mixture into small balls and coat
each in carob powder, coconut or cocoa. Store balls in the
refrigerator. Makes 24 balls.

Vary this recipe by substituting another nut butter, such as
almond paste (additive-free paste is available commercially), for
the peanut butter.

Peanut (Soya Bean) Butter Slice

½ cup peanut butter (sugar-free commercial kind or make your own, see recipe p. 90) or soya-bean butter (see recipe p. 89)
1 tablespoon honey or 2 teaspoons fructose or Equal to taste (optional)
2½-3½ tablespoons goat's or soya milk powder
½ cup chopped raisins
coconut or toasted sesame seeds for coating

Cream the peanut butter, adding sweetener (if used), and work in the milk powder gradually, using enough to make a stiff dough. Knead in raisins evenly, then roll into a 2½ cm (1 in) diameter by 25 cm (10 in) long log. Coat the roll in coconut or toasted sesame seeds, chill and then slice. Alternatively, roll the mixture into balls and roll each in coconut or toasted sesame seeds. Store the slice or balls in the refrigerator.

Eating Chocolate

3-4 tablespoons carob or 2 tablespoons cocoa to taste
1 cup soya milk or goat's milk powder
1½ cups coconut and/or mixed dried fruit
¼ cup chopped nuts (optional)
2 teaspoons fructose or honey (optional)
250 g (8 oz) melted copha

Sift the carob or cocoa with the milk powder into a bowl, then stir in the coconut or dried fruit and nuts and sweetener (if used). Pour the copha over the mixture and mix well. Turn into a 28 by 18 cm (11 by 7 in) slab tin and cut into small squares before the chocolate sets too hard. Store chocolate in the refrigerator—the flavour improves with overnight refrigeration.

Protein Snack

    1 beaten egg
    ¾ cup roasted and ground peanuts
    ¾ cup coconut
    1½ tablespoons water
    3 teaspoons soya bean oil
    1½ tablespoons soya flour or soya milk powder

Add the rest of the ingredients to the egg and mix well; adjust
the consistency with extra flour or coconut if necessary. Roll
the mixture into balls or form into a log and coat with coconut;
store in the refrigerator. Makes about 20 slices.

    The following two carob recipes may be made with cocoa
if carob is not tolerated.

Carob-coated Nuts 'n' Raisins

    4 teaspoons margarine
    125 g (4 oz) melted copha
    8 tablespoons carob powder (sifted if lumpy)
    whole nuts and dried fruit

Add the margarine to the copha and stir over heat till melted
and well blended—do not boil or overheat. Pour the mixture
over the carob powder in a small bowl and stir till well mixed.
Allow the mixture to cool until slightly thickened, then dip the
nuts and fruit into the mixture and coat evenly. Remove them
with tongs and place on a sheet of greaseproof paper on a plate
and chill to set; store in the refrigerator.

    Clusters may be made by placing several nuts and dried
fruits together in tiny paper cases. If using paper cases there is
no need to allow the mixture to thicken. Simply spoon the
mixture over the nuts and fruit so that it runs between them
and fills up the spaces, and then set in the refrigerator.

    Makes 1⅓ cups of mixture; each paper case takes 2 tea-
spoons of mixture.

Carob Clusters

½ cup warm water
2 tablespoons margarine
⅓ cup goat's or soya milk powder
3 tablespoons carob powder
2 tablespoons lecithin granules
1 cup nuts or raw or roasted peanuts
1 cup currants or chopped raisins

Place the water, margarine, milk and carob powders and lecithin in a blender and process until smooth. Pour the carob mixture over the nuts and dried fruit in a large bowl and mix until coated evenly. Spoon the mixture into patty cases forming clumps—tiny petit-four cases are ideal for this. Place on trays in a cold oven, turn oven to 150°C (300°F) and heat for 10-15 minutes or until clusters have started to dry out. Remove from oven and leave clusters in the open to dry out further—this may take a few hours. Makes about 36 clusters.

Allergy-free Icy-poles

Inexpensive icy-pole moulds may be purchased from department and chain stores and some supermarkets. More than one set is desirable if there are several children in your family, or neighbourhood, as I find that all children, whether they have food allergies or not, like the following icy-poles. They are quick to make and form a healthy treat on a hot day. Paddle-pop sticks may be purchased in inexpensive packets from toy and craft shops or department stores—they are useful as extra icy-pole sticks. Icy-poles are also an excellent way to use up left-over milkshakes, milk toppings, etcetera, as the following ideas will show:

• Squeeze fresh fruit juices or use your juice extractor—orange, apple, pineapple and pear are all good. A little passion-fruit pulp can be stirred into the prepared juice, especially with citrus juices, but do not put passionfruit into a blender or a juice extractor. Mix the juices for a fruit-salad effect.

- A "surprise" fruit icy-pole may be made by placing a small piece of fruit—banana (delicious frozen) and watermelon are effective—in the bottom of the icy-pole mould. If long sticks are used (such as paddle-pop sticks), push the stick into the fruit and then pour the liquid over the top. This enables the stick to stay centred in the liquid.
- Mash some banana with a little orange juice and add goat's or soya milk, or goat's yoghurt, and mix thoroughly.
- Protein Shake (see recipe p. 22).
- Left-over Banana Topping (see recipe p. 173) or other frozen fruit topping.
- Custard-based icy-poles: use the plain custard recipe on p. 46; add mashed banana with a little lemon or orange juice, or some carob powder or cocoa.

As an alternative to icy-poles, iced fruit pieces may be prepared very quickly: simply cut oranges into segments and freeze (with skin on)—they make the most "natural" orange ice-blocks; or remove seedless grapes from stems, and wash and freeze them whole—they are also very refreshing to suck on a hot day.

INDEX OF EGG-FREE RECIPES

Egg substitutes in baking are given on pages 15 and 16. These may be used to make your own favourite recipes egg-free.

207

INDEX OF MILK-FREE RECIPES

The recipes in this index are totally milk-free, that is, they contain neither goat's, soya, nor, of course, cow's milk. Other recipes in this book that stipulate goat's milk may be made dairy-free by substituting soya milk, fruit juice or other liquid options (see, for example, page 75 for some ideas).

INDEX OF SWEETENER-FREE RECIPES

For those people unable to tolerate any form of added sweetener, the recipes in this index contain no sweeteners, that is, no fructose, honey, Equal or extra sultanas liquefied with a liquid ingredient.

For those not so restricted, suitable options are given with other recipes in this book.

GENERAL INDEX

212

213